MODEL CITY PYONGYANG

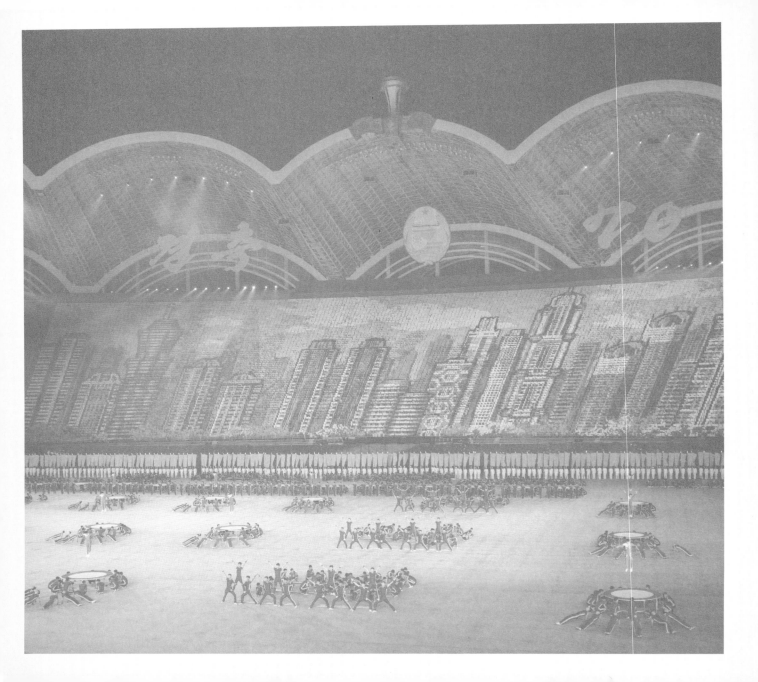

Cristiano Bianchi • Kristina Drapić

MODEL CITY PYONGYANG

Foreword by Pico Iyer • In collaboration with Koryo Studio

The MIT Press | Cambridge, Massachusetts

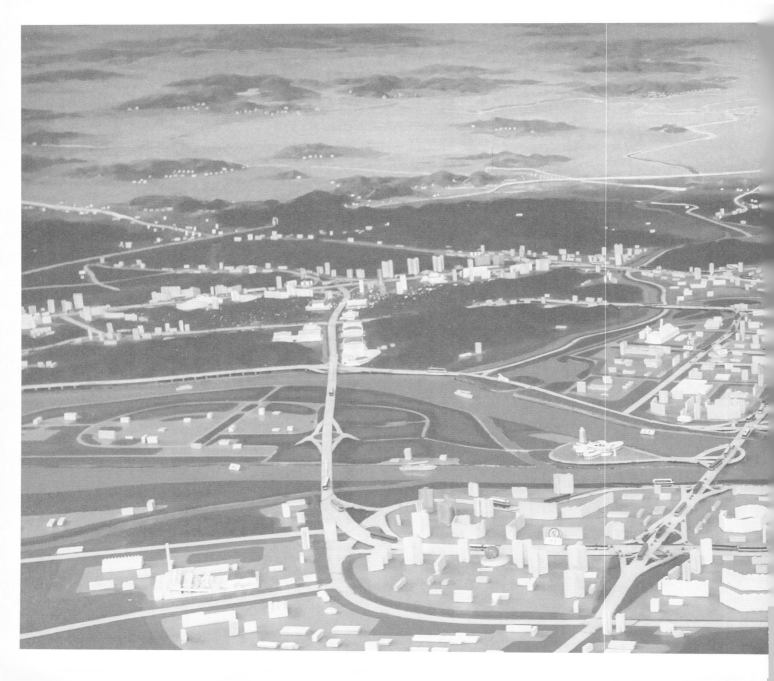

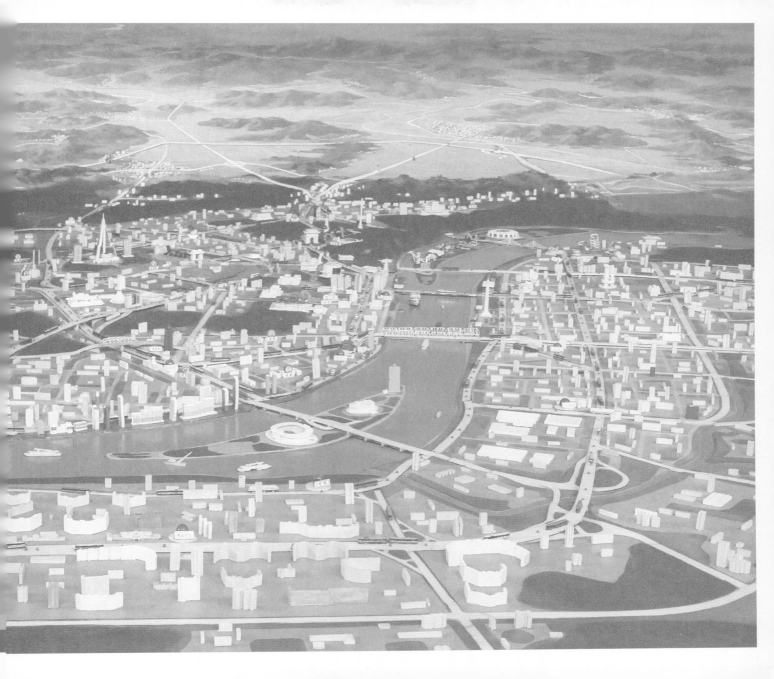

The Blueprint of Blueprints Pico Iyer

As I walked around the Paektusan Academy of Architecture in Pyongyang some years ago, I couldn't help but be struck by the photographs of all the great buildings across the globe, from the ancient world to right now. Architecture students everywhere learn from the masters, but here I got the sense that the bright young designers of North Korea's capital were being encouraged to not only reproduce the wonders of the world, but to make them bigger, better, newer. If you can replicate everything everyone else has made – and then surpass it – how can anyone possibly call you backward?

That, I think, is the logic of the Land of the Kims, which has taken planning and its public face – architecture – to their most dramatic extremes. Drive around the showpiece city, past the Arch of Triumph, 10 m (33 ft) taller than the one in Paris, and gleaming sports centres and cinemas, and you can easily feel as if you're inside an architectural blueprint: everything looks the way it was meant to look, and the spotless, often car-less, boulevards seem to lack nothing but signs of life.

We all know that the Democratic People's Republic of Korea is, to an astonishing extent, the work of one master-builder and his family, yet I am often shocked at how little most of us in the West know about daily life in this nation of 25 million, and the notions that lie behind its jaw-dropping structures. At best, we have heard of the 105-storey tourist hotel shaped like a rocket ship (opposite), the dazzling subway stations, the amusement parks and the space-age theatres, but until thumbing through the pages of this book, I'd never known the symbolism behind the larger design scheme and the way, for example, the monumental statues are built to face the rising sun.

This is one reason I am grateful for the deconstruction in this book of the axes of the city, its optical illusions and its God's-eye messages. With a country known almost solely through rumours and opinions, nothing could be more welcome than receiving what we get here: a neutral, concrete and architecturally precise explication of Pyongyang's literal foundations, and of the surreal constructions erected out of what was, only 65 years ago, mostly rubble.

I will never forget the first time I visited Kim Il Sung's land in 1990. While in Beijing, I happened to be walking past a large, seemingly deserted building, with pictures and yet more pictures of the Great Leader along the gates at the entrance.

good impression. The beauty of seeing the city in the flesh lies in getting a glimpse of something human behind all the brutalist statues and theories. Those three slot machines in the basement of the Yanggakdo International Hotel – what were they all about? Those friendly strangers on the subway cars, who struck up a cheery conversation with me in English – were they just for show, actors hired by the government to impersonate regular folks? How many of the rooms in those illuminated skyscrapers were actually occupied? Nothing I had read before about North Korea had prepared me for a world that raised as many questions as conclusions.

This was useful to me, as I have never had much time for Stalinist ideologies, and had seen what similar systems had wrought in Lhasa, Hanoi and Yangon. Yet North Korea has taken the Marxist–Leninist handbook and executed every precept to perfection, while infusing the end product with its own particular brand of nationalism and fanaticism. Over regular visits to Cuba from 1987 to 2013, I marvelled at the beauty and fading glory of its collapsing structures. Pyongyang, with its immaculate streets, perfectly maintained halls and displays of public unity, couldn't have been more different. In a curious way, its discipline and stress on community-mindedness reminded me of Japan, a country where I have lived for more than 30 years.

The 20th century was, of course, a great time for model cities, from Oscar Niemeyer's Brasília to Le Corbusier's Chandigarh; the Disney town of Celebration, Florida, to such postmodern confections as Dubai. Modern Shanghai clearly takes its inspiration from a source not so different from the North Korean capital. Once when I flew to Pyongyang from Las Vegas (via San Francisco, Osaka and Beijing), I was struck by the similarity between the two manufactured utopias, for all their extreme differences in values and direction. Of course, the North Korean capital is, in part, a showcase city, which citizens are encouraged to visit, and be awed by, but where only a privileged few are permitted to live. As an expression of scale (sometimes displacing: look at the statues in relation to the humans bowing before them) and as a rare city built to be seen from on high, Pyongyang is not a place that any visitor is likely to forget.

Deducing that this must be the North Korean embassy, I walked in to present my British passport to a desk officer. His country enjoyed no diplomatic relations with Great Britain, he explained, but I was welcome to visit. If I came back in three days, he would make available to me a budget, mid-price or luxury tour, for three days, five or seven. I returned 72 hours later, and he was as good as his word. Very soon I was walking around Pyongyang with an intelligent and English-fluent guide who had spent four years seeing the world outside North Korea, while mastering Urdu in Pakistan.

That was my first taste of how desperately the regime is in need of hard currency – and of how keen it is to make a

Within the pages of this book we finally get a clear, careful spelling-out of the thinking behind the façades. One can be appalled by what the North Korean system represents, and still be amazed by the extent to which it marshals human endeavour to create a two-dimensional foreground more flawless than any I have seen in Guangzhou or Tokyo or Seoul. All of those places have quite a lot in common with Pyongyang in terms of their theme-park sensibility and readiness to see a replica of something as no less powerful than the thing itself, but none has gone as far as the capital of the DPRK in realizing one man's vision. It is hard not to wonder what these people could achieve if given the opportunity and resources.

I still remember the streets of Beijing as I saw them in 1985; to a remarkable degree, they looked and felt like Pyongyang today, though without the eerily uninhabited high-rises that have become the latter's spooky calling card. On my most recent visit, I walked around the ten million square feet (about 929,000 m²) ghost town that is the Pyongyang Film Studio and saw the locally cherished movie, *Chongchuniyo! (O Youth!)*, screened by its director in a plush, red-velvet screening room worthy of Beverly Hills. The effect was akin to going to a mega-church, pulsing with full-throated affirmations. The faith left me cold, but it was hard not to be struck by the building and the dedication of the choir.

In North Korea, it is famously difficult to tell where fantasy ends and real life begins. But upon my most recent return to the country, I was struck by the presence of not just a 36-lane bowling alley and pizza parlours, but also mobile phones, which, for all the restrictions placed on them, may eventually let fragments of the real world in. Even though everything a visitor sees and hears is curated, it still makes the faraway country breathe a little easier to hear a guide with a white Chanel clip in her hair talk about her problems as an unmarried woman of 26, or to see a North Korean cross-question an Apple product manager about how Tim Cook's vision differs from that of Steve Jobs.

Even such orchestrated scraps are more alive than anything you can get from a distance, and more complex than any video available on YouTube – one reason why I always urge friends to visit the countries that are only dark spaces in our minds, or to take the first step by inspecting Liberation Street or Unification Street in a book such as this. At some point, North Korea is going to be forced to join the larger world, and then these buildings may no longer be mere display-cases or advertisements, but places where people live. The more we turn away from such cities, the more we are condemned to a murderous ignorance – and the more their people are condemned to the horrors of solitary confinement.

The Model City
Cristiano Bianchi and Kristina Drapić

We visited Pyongyang for the first time in July 2015, with the support of Koryo Studio, which later gave us full access to its archive, library and art collection, and returned the following year, this time with the support of Korea Cities Federation, to further our study of the city's architecture and meet architects and professors at the University of Architecture and Building Materials. During a final trip in 2018 to complete the photography, we were granted access to buildings not normally open to foreigners, many of which have never been published.

After our first visit, Nick Bonner of Koryo Studio asked us if we, as architects, thought Pyongyang was beautiful. It was a simple question, yet difficult – if not impossible – to answer. Our first reaction was of embarrassed protests, but once we let go of our view of the European ideal, we realized that the city did have its own strange kind of beauty. Pyongyang embodies the dream of total planning, to which every architect secretly aspires: jettisoning planning restrictions, space-ratio guidelines, land costs and all of the other constraints that govern modern architecture, and returning to the idea of a city of the people, in which everything is designed in a single, cohesive vision.

The idea of designing a 'model city' for a new kind of society recurs throughout the history of architecture – an ambition shared by political leaders and architects alike. Model cities have been envisioned and built over the centuries, from the Renaissance planned towns of Pienza and Ferrara to the Modernist utopias of Brasília and Chandigarh. Pyongyang is one of these. But owing to the isolation of the country, access to this open-air museum of socialist architecture has been limited. While most of these model cities were superimposed on an existing urban fabric, or later transformed by different ideological contexts, Pyongyang is a unique example of an urban centre that was completely planned and rebuilt after a single event – the Korean War (1950–53) – and developed under one vision: the peculiar state ideology known as 'Juche'.

On Architecture, written in 1991 by Kim Jong Il (1941–2011), the second Supreme Leader of North Korea, describes the importance of architecture for the political power of a country, and provides ideological and practical guidance on how to build a city that communicates ideas to its citizens through its buildings. Many of the rules outlined in these pages were applied across Pyongyang, evident not only in the city's plan,

which is dominated by axis and symmetry, but also in its skyline. Every building was, and is, built by the state, often with the shape and height specially designed to frame a particular space or view, from the residential blocks that form a symmetrical background to the Juche Tower to the recent development of Ryomyong Street, with its progression of towers echoing the shape of a mountain, positioned perfectly on the axis of the Three Revolutions Exhibition.

One of our aims during this project was to document those buildings of Pyongyang that still retained their original design scheme. A massive renovation programme, beginning in 2012, led to the redesign of many important structures, with the overriding strategy guided seemingly by a desire for uniformity, rather than conservation. Glass façades with their bronze frames have been replaced by highly reflective curtain walls, while inside, terrazzo floors and mosaics made way for vast expanses of sterile marble, and the overall decoration greatly simplified. As a result, the character of each building has been reduced to a version of 'international modern', or a garishly colourful environment showcasing the latest architectural advances.

This disregard for the old and embracing of the new is not uncommon in Asian cultures, but is at odds with the Western tradition of heritage and preservation. On a visit to the Paektusan Academy of Architecture, we met one of ten Korean architects sent in the early 2000s to Italy to study architecture. He told us that when he returned home, he had suggested applying the conservation-led methods they had learned, but quickly realized such ideas were too alien for Korean sensibilities. We decided that it was important to photograph buildings in their original condition wherever we could, but in some cases, we were too late: the gorgeous, brutalist International Cinema Hall was supposed to be one of the highlights of this book, but building works began a few weeks before we planned to photograph it (in 2016), and we were not allowed to enter. When we returned two years later, the concrete façade had been covered in white and grey tiles.

In 2016 the Pyongyang Ice Rink still retained its original design, inside and out. When we arrived to photograph it, the management, mortified by the poor condition, asked us not to photograph the cracks in the floor. When we said that these signs of use were both normal, given the building's age, and beautiful, they looked puzzled and said that we were unlucky as it was going to be renovated soon, and we could have photographed the new design had we come later. Before we left, we were asked for our thoughts on how best to proceed with the renovation. 'Preserve everything!' we said. 'Repair it, but don't change it!' This was accompanied by guffaws of laughter at what they thought was a joke.

This book is the result of an amazing experience, an immersion into a different world. It is a visual journey through the city's architecture and urban spaces. Rather than taking a purely documentary approach, we chose to communicate what we saw and the impressions we later digested through

Federation. Problems did arise: we were denied access to buildings at the last minute, despite having submitted the photography list months before, and the schedule was reshuffled each day because of last-minute changes in permissions. Bad weather also led to rescheduling shoots.

In addition, we had to stick to some iron-clad rules: we could not crop images of the leaders or their slogans, and had to photograph residential buildings from a certain distance (not too close). We had to ask permission before photographing people, and we couldn't photograph the military at all. Sometimes we couldn't even cross the road to get a better angle – although why this should be so was unclear. It was very important that we followed these strictures, as our guides would be held responsible for our actions. By understanding this, and accepting the rules as part of the experience of this different reality, we earned the trust of our guides, and consequently a degree of freedom, along with small concessions that could make all the difference in getting a good shot.

our photographs. Many foreigners visiting Pyongyang for the first time find it difficult to get to grips with both the built environment and how society interacts with it. They arrive to find a city that is part theatre, part reality, and completely alien to their own experience of urban life.

We wanted to capture this feeling of 'fictional reality' by following the techniques used by Korean artists when depicting the supreme leaders or sacred places. We were fascinated by the striking way in which the sky is represented in art and propaganda – sometimes a simple gradient of colours; sometimes a hyper-saturated sunset or sunrise. In homage to this, our photographs combine classic architectural views of buildings with skies represented by gradients of pastel colours. The contrast between the two halves creates a visual alienation, where the real becomes unreal and the unreal becomes real. Fact is fiction; fiction becomes fact.

Getting approval for the project wasn't too difficult – Koreans are very proud of their architecture – but arranging permissions and access had to be carefully organized, largely in advance, and with a great deal of hard work and patience. For this we owe a huge debt to Koryo Studio and Korea Cities

Why we decided to engage in a cultural project in the DPRK in the first place is not an easy question to answer. At first, it was simple curiosity, followed by a growing feeling of being intrigued by such an unknown subject. We soon discovered that our interest was sometimes seen with suspicion, as many outsiders agree with the logic of sanctions, boycott and isolation. People would often ask questions to confirm their own prejudices and preconceptions, rather than to learn something new. For ourselves, we remain convinced that isolation doesn't benefit anyone, and that art and architecture can serve as an important means of cultural exchange, regardless of boundaries. By sharing our experience of exploring, and then understanding, something different, we aim to open a window onto a different culture, and to reveal, through the architecture of Pyongyang, a different kind of beauty.

MONUMENTAL SPACE

Pyongyang's 'monumental space' is dictated by a set of strict compositional guidelines, codified in *On Architecture* by Kim Jong Il. A building's value, he wrote, is defined by its ideological content, so these guidelines set out a comprehensive narrative, comprising four principles (overleaf) that can be applied across different scales, represented here by the City Centre (p. 22), Kim Il Sung Square (p. 26) and the Mansu Hill Grand Monument (p. 32).

Principles of the Monumental Space

Focus: Based around a central element, usually a statue or portrait of the leader, or a symbol of Juche, the state ideology. The surrounding space must not detract from it. Size is also important, as it reinforces the ideological content.

Background: The purpose of the background is to control the three-dimensional quality of the monumental space, blocking anything behind the focal point, and redirect attention onto it. It forms the 'backdrop' to the scene being played out in front of it.

Framing: Reinforcing the focal point with symmetrical elements on either side concentrates attention and provides balance to achieve the essential atmosphere of respect and dignity.

Projection: One side of the monumental space is left open to project the scene's ideological content out to the horizon, symbolizing the future.

City Centre

The focal point of the City Centre is Kim Il Sung Square, the political and cultural heart of the city. The background is defined by Namsan, the hill rising behind it, and a collection of highrise residential buildings. It is framed by two symmetrical bridges: Okryu to the north, and Taedong to the south. The framing on the Okryu side is reinforced by the massive presence of the new tower complexes that line Changion Street, completed in 2012, which increase in height as they progress towards the river, echoing the shape of the two sculptural groups on either side of the Mansu Hill Grand Monument. As the major monumental spaces are traditionally orientated towards the rising sun, the City Centre is projected towards the east, with an open view of the mountains beyond.

Mural in the Mangyongdae Children's Palace

Kim Il Sung Square

The Tribune Building provides the focus of the square, with portraits of Kim Il Sung and Kim Jong Il on its façade, and is where Kim Jong Un stands during official events and celebrations. Behind it is the Grand People's Study House, which distils traditional Korean architectural forms into a massive public building across 10 floors, with a library, reading rooms, lecture halls and services. The square is bordered on two sides by four neoclassical buildings, with the headquarters of the Workers' Party of Korea and the Korean Art Gallery facing the Ministry of Foreign Trade and the Korean Central History Museum. The view to the east looks out to Juche Tower, about 800 m (2,625 ft) away. While standing in the square, the tower appears to emerge from it; in reality, it is on the opposite bank of the Taedong River, an optical effect achieved with the aid of a raised platform.

Rehearsal for a mass torchlight parade in the square

Kim Il Sung Square

Mansu Hill Grand Monument

The focus here is fixed firmly on two bronze statues of Kim Il Sung (sculpted in 1972, on the occasion of his 60th birthday) and Kim Jong Il (added in 2012, one year after his death), each 22 m (72 ft) in height. Behind them, forming the background, is the Korean Revolution Museum, the façade of which displays a mosaic mural depicting Mount Paektu. Framing the scene are two symmetrical sculptural groups, also in bronze: *Liberation from Japanese Rule*, to mark the end of Japanese occupation in 1945, and *Achievements of Socialism*, a celebration of the Socialist Revolution. The sculptures feature 119 and 109 figures, respectively, clustered around two flags, 50 m (164 ft) in length and 23 m (75 ft) in height. The view is open to the east, towards the Monument to Party Founding and the Juche Tower.

타도제국주의

Axis 1 Mansu Hill Grand Monument to the Monument to Party Founding

At 2.1 km (1.3 miles), the axis from the Mansu Hill Grand Monument to the Monument to Party Founding is so long that on a hazy day you can barely see from one end to the other. The shape of the two residential buildings flanking the Monument to Party Founding echoes the flags held aloft by the sculptural groups in front of the Mansu Hill Grand Monument at the opposite end of the axis (overleaf). The buildings were originally white, but later painted red to reinforce the connection; on their rooftops are characters that spell out the words 'a hundred battles, a hundred victories'. Serving as an extension of the axis is the Ryugyong Hotel, 1.8 km (1 mile) from the Mansu Hill Grand Monument, which rises like a massive futuristic pyramid from the city below.

Monument to Party Founding

Monument to Party Founding

Axis 2   Kim Il Sung Square to the Juche Tower

The axis from Kim Il Sung Square to Juche Tower is 0.8 km (0.5 miles) long, and continues, unfinished, behind the tower for other 1.3 km (0.8 miles). Already visible in the first plans for the reconstruction of Pyongyang – produced in 1951, two years before the end of the Korean War – it marks the geographic and symbolic centre of the city. The square was completed in 1954, and enlarged in 1987; its western end, the Grand People's Study House (opposite), was completed in 1982. The progressively decreasing heights of buildings on the other side of the river provide a frame for the Juche Tower (pp. 48–49). In *On Architecture*, Kim Jong Il describes this symmetry as necessary to achieving balance and sense of dignity within the monumental space, allowing it to perform its primary function of expressing an ideological content.

Kim Il Sung Square

Juche Tower

Axis 3   Potong Gate to the Ryugyong Hotel

The axis between the 6th-century Potong Gate and the futuristic Ryugyong Hotel – one from the past and one representing an as yet unrealized future – is a metaphor for varying ideas about scale and monumentality. Once the western entry point to the ancient walled city, the Potong Gate was destroyed and rebuilt three times (in 997, 1473 and 1955). It originally sat on the imperial highway connecting Seoul and Beijing, and is where the six-year-old Kim Il Sung saw protesters killed by Japanese police in 1919. At the opposite end of the axis is the enigmatic, almost sci-fi Ryugyong Hotel, with its huge glass-encased concrete shell piercing the sky. Conceived as a mixed-use structure, it was designed to indicate a desire for internationalism and openness – similar, in fact, to what happened in China in the 1980s under Deng Xiaoping, when hotels were used as testing grounds for change.

Ryugyong Hotel

Ryugyong Hotel

Potong Gate

Ryugyong Hotel

CITIES WITHIN THE CITY

Large complexes of public buildings are grouped along Pyongyang's monumental axes, including the Three Revolutions Exhibition (City of Culture; p. 58), in the Ryonmot-dong area, and Chongchun Street (City of Sports; p. 66), and were conceived as individual 'cities within the city'. The architecture of the buildings is highly symbolic, designed with the express purpose of allowing each building to be clearly identified.

City of Culture   Three Revolutions Exhibition

This cultural complex is the official showcase of Kim Il Sung's three revolutions –
ideological, technical and cultural, the guiding precepts of the Workers' Party
of Korea. The Three Revolutions Exhibition began life as the Industrial and
Agricultural Exhibition in 1946, which lasted until 1956. It was developed into
its current incarnation in 1983, before being greatly enlarged and modernized
10 years later. The complex comprises six buildings, with a total area of 80,000 m²
(over 860,000 sq ft), lining the east and west sides of a 750 m (2,460 ft)-long,
100 m (328 ft)-wide axis. Their massive scale emphasizes the importance of the
exhibits inside, while the individual logos at the top of each building reflect
the ideological content within.

Electronics Industry Hall
Area: 10,000 m² (107,640 sq ft)

Objects on display are related
to the electronics and automation
industries, communication
and space research, robotics,
computers, optical and measuring
instruments. The building also
contains a planetarium and section
devoted to research into the
peaceful use of atomic energy.

Light Industry Hall (ill. p. 59)
Area: 15,000 m² (161,460 sq ft)

Exhibits here cover pharmaceuticals,
medicine, food processing, furniture,
homeware, shoes, textiles and
cosmetics, city management and
the prevention of industrial pollution,
with a focus on the development and
production of fabrics woven from
handmade fibres.

Agricultural Hall
Area: 10,000 m² (107,640 sq ft)

Farming methods and machinery
form the emphasis here, along
with fertilizers, livestock farming,
mariculture, tideland reclamation,
land management, fishing,
hydrometeorology, oceanography,
seismology. There is also a section
devoted to Antarctic expeditions.

**New Technology
Development Hall**
Area: 10,000 m² (107,640 sq ft)

Exhibits in this building are
devoted to domestic inventions and
achievements in new technology.
It is not open to foreigners.

Heavy Industry Hall
Area: 23,000 m² (247,570 sq ft)

Items related to mining,
metalworking and shipbuilding
are on display here, as well as the
construction, transport and machine
industries, land development and
transportation. There is also a
section devoted to the production
of iron and steel from domestic
raw materials.

**General Introduction Hall
(overleaf)**
Area: 11,000 m² (118,400 sq ft)

Exhibits here are focused on the
achievements of the ideological
and cultural revolution, including
works written by the leaders,
the development of the socialist
educational system, and the social
sciences, arts, literature, cinema,
sports and healthcare.

City of Sports Chongchun Street

The culture of sports and sporting activities, already important to the Koreans, was widely encouraged during the development of the new socialist society. The 'City of Sports' complex on Chongchun Street comprises 10 indoor gymnasiums and a football stadium, a hotel, health centre, restaurants and other facilities. Construction began in 1988 for the 13th World Festival of Youth and Students, held in Pyongyang the following year, and was completed in 1996. Like those that form the Three Revolutions Exhibition, each building in the City of Sports has an individual identity, although they are linked visually by the formal brutalism of the architecture. The design of the individual structures was led by, and in turn communicates, the activities that take place inside.

Handball Hall
Area: 10,148 m² (109,232 sq ft)
Seats: 2,400

A recent renovation has closed
off the row of windows at the front
of the hall and reduced the diagonal
gash of windows on the side. The
lower section has been repainted
a dark red, and the logo made more
stylized, and less realistic.

Taekwondo Hall
Area: 17,740 m² (1,909,512 sq ft)
Seats: 2,400

As the sport of taekwondo is a blend
of traditional martial arts, the hall
features the curved roof and ceramic
tiles more often seen on the country's
historic buildings. The lettering
on the front spells out 'taekwondo'
in Kim Jong Il's handwriting.

Volleyball Hall
Area: 12,250 m² (131,860 sq ft)
Seats: 2,000

The interior of this building, one
of the most visited by tourists in
Pyongyang, has recently been
renovated by using sound-absorbing
materials for the walls and the
ceiling and a palette of pastel
colours for the floor and seats.

Sosan Football Stadium
Area: 11,700
Seats: 25,000

The Sosan Stadium is mostly used
for football, the most popular sport
in the DPRK, and also hosts track
events. Major matches are played at
Kim il Sung or Yanggakdo stadiums.

Weightlifting Hall
Area: 7,180 m² (77,285 sq ft)
Seats: 2,000

Like many of the buildings on
Chongchun Street, the design was
guided by the activities taking place
inside; in this case, the weights on
a barbell. The interior was featured
in *Chongchuniyo! (O Youth!)*.

Badminton Hall
Area: 6,300 m² (67,813 sq ft)
Seats: 3,000

The arena retains its original design
concept, based on a shuttlecock,
of an octagonal plan, with stands
surrounding the playing courts.

Indoor Swimming Pool
Area: 23,605 m² (254,082 sq ft)
Seats: 3,400

During renovations, the original
glass façade with bronze framing
was replaced by a mirrored green
curtain wall. The logo previously
featured a stylized representation
of the ocean waves.

Wrestling Hall
Area: 10,000 m² (107,640 sq ft)
Seats: 2,300

Recent renovations has meant
the removal of the glass façade at
either side of the entrance, as well
as the perforated concrete screen
above. The logo has also been
changed from the original design
of two boxing gloves.

Table Tennis Hall (opposite)
Area: 18,246 m² (196,400 sq ft)
Seats: 4,300

Like the Wrestling Hall (p. 75),
the original transparent glass and
bronze frame has been replaced
by a curtain wall of reflective glazing.
The logo has also changed slightly.
The building's design is based on the
net used in table tennis.

Basketball Hall
Area: 9,905 m² (106,617 sq ft)
Seats: 2,000

The interior was originally
illuminated by windows, and
appears in the film *Chongchuniyo!*
(O Youth!). During renovations these
glazed openings were removed, and
the fabric covering the walls was
replaced with wooden panels.

Athletics Stadium (overleaf)
Area: 22,766 m² (245,050 sq ft)
Seats: 4,000

Here, too, the glass to either side
of the entrance was removed during
renovations, as was a perforated
concrete screen above. The logo
of a ribbon in the shape of a flower
has also been changed.

SOCIAL CONDENSERS

Pyongyang's residential highrises were designed and built according to the Soviet constructivist theory of 'social condensers', which suggests that the design itself defines the behaviour of its residents. The apartment building, therefore, becomes the stage set for a new kind of society.

Kwangbok Street

Kwangbok ('Liberation') Street is one of the most ambitious residential projects in Pyongyang. Completed in 1989 on the occasion of the World Festival of Youth and Students, and comprising around 260 buildings and 25,000 apartments, it is viewed as a huge success in providing housing to an unprecedented number of people. The enormous highrises with 30, 35 or 42 storeys, designed in different configurations (Triple Cylinder, Double Y, Bar, and so on), are mainly home to members of the bureaucratic and cultural institutions of the DPRK. They are placed at regular intervals, connected by an almost continuous strip of lowrise structures. The vast size of the buildings and the distances between them (the street is about 120 m [394 ft] wide) result in an overwhelming sense of scale that contrasts with the ordinary events of everyday life happening below at street level.

Double Y

Bar

Windmill

Tongil Street

Tongil ('Reunification') Street, completed in 1992, is a residential development in the southern area of the city, located at the start of the Pyongyang–Kaesong Highway, leading to the DMZ, the de facto border with South Korea (not recognized by either country). Upon entering the city through the Arch of Reunification, Tongil Street gives the impression of vast space, and features some of the largest buildings of the city – up to 85,000 m^2 (915,000 sq ft), and housing around 2,000 people – and the widest stretch of road (about 200 m, or 656 ft). Unlike Kwangbok Street (pp. 82–95), the architecture is simpler and less varied, without the distinct building typologies of the former, giving a more austere appearance to the urban landscape. This austerity has been softened by repainting some of the façades in pink, blue and green, from their original colour scheme of all white.

Residential Projects

Along with the large complexes of Kwangbok (pp. 82–95) and Tongil (pp. 96–101) streets, Pyongyang is also dotted with smaller residential buildings. Some are highly unusual in their configuration, such as the condominium on Sungri Street, which has two wings that curve in different directions (p. 104), while others were designed to frame a particular monument, in this case the Monument to Party Founding (pp. 108–9). Still others sport slogans on their rooftops (pp. 106–7), or incorporate elements from traditional Korean architecture (p. 115). The concrete façades were painted in vivid pastel shades in the 1990s under Kim Jong Il, a practice that has been continued – and accelerated – by Kim Jong Un, saturating the panoramic view of the city with colour.

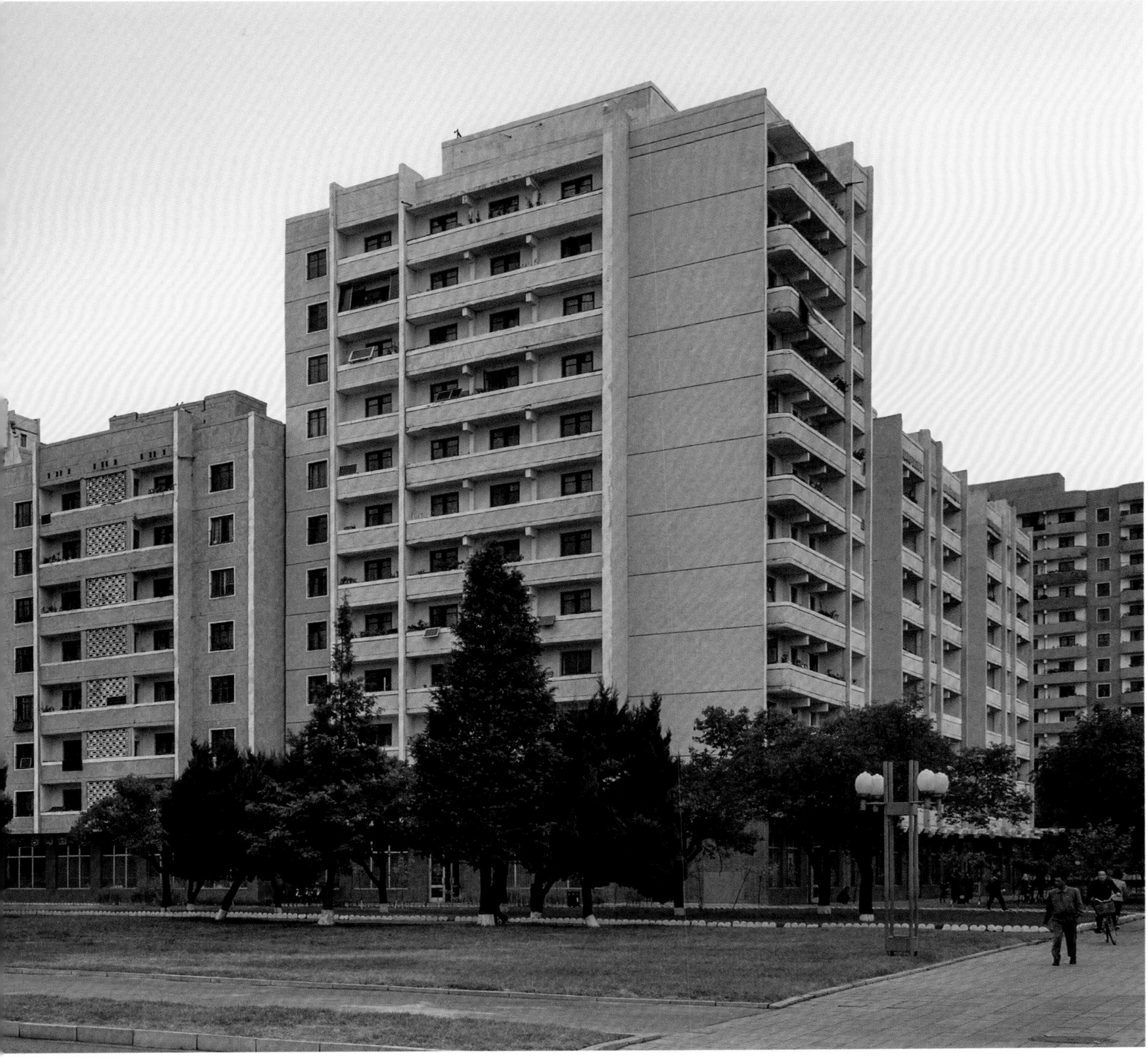

Munsu Street

Changgwang Street

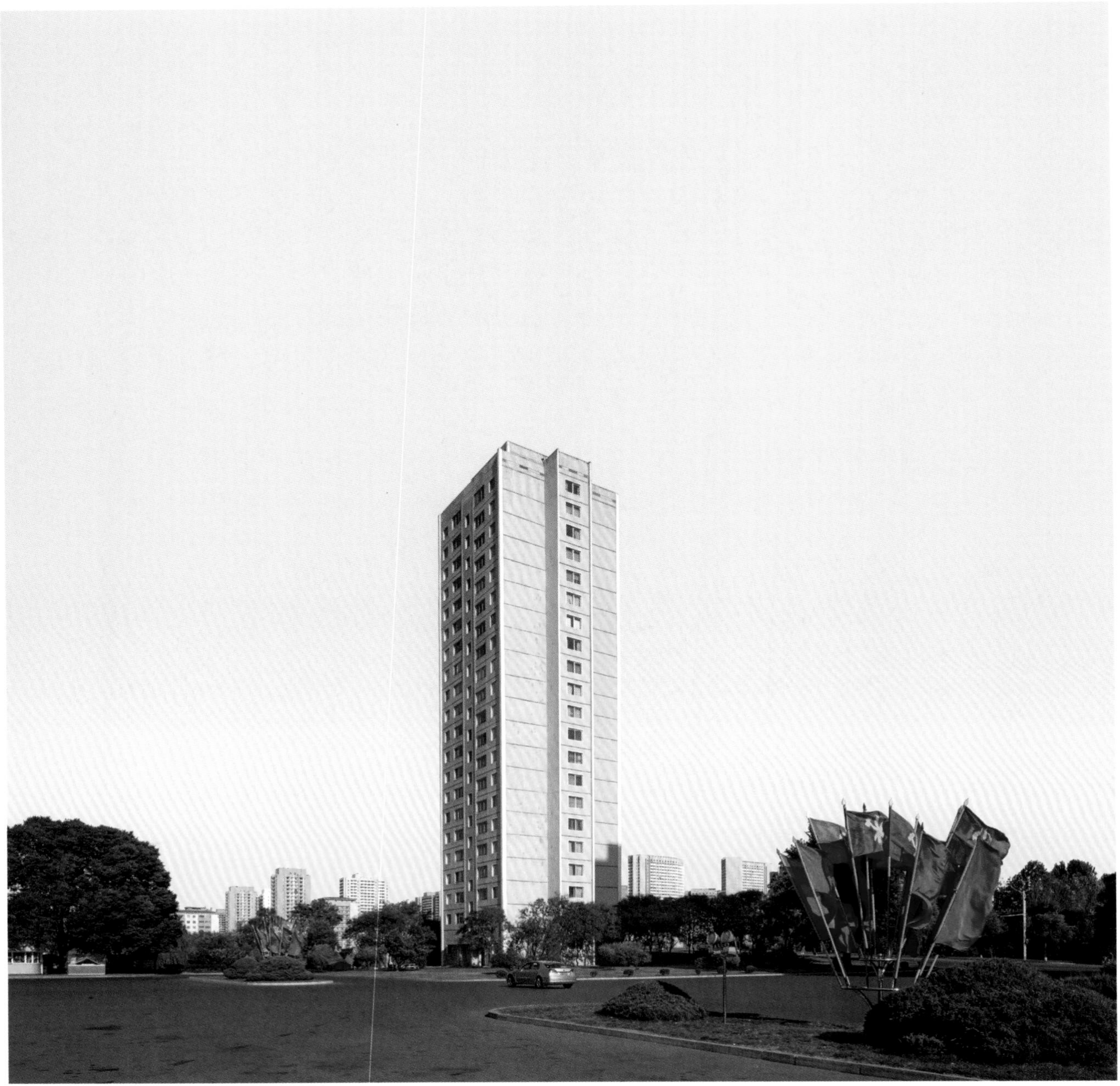

ICONS

The cityscape of Pyongyang is filled with buildings that are potent with symbolism and have become iconic works of architecture – even beyond the confines of the DPRK. These public and semi-public buildings – from government headquarters to museums, libraries, sporting arenas and hotels – are highly individual, instantly recognizable, and essential to the visual narrative of the city.

Tower of Eternal Life
Location: Kumsong Street
Date: 1997
Height: 92 m (302 ft)

Built to honour the 'eternal life' of
Kim Il Sung. Two arches span the six
lanes leading from the city centre
to the Kumsusan Palace of the Sun
(p. 123), so that people going to pay
their respects to the leaders must
pass beneath the tower.

Arch of Triumph
Location: Moran Hill
Date: 1982
Height: 60 m (197 ft)

Constructed from 25,550 blocks of granite (marking each day lived by Kim Il Sung as of his 70th birthday), the monument sits on the spot where he gave his first address in 1945, marking the end of Japanese occupation.

Arch of Reunification (overleaf)
Location: Reunification Highway
Date: 2001
Height: 30 m (98 ft)

Commemorates the reunification proposals put forward by Kim Il Sung. It shows two Korean women in traditional dress, symbolizing the North and the South, leaning forward to jointly uphold a sphere bearing a map of a reunified Korea.

Indoor Stadium
Location: Chollima Street
Date: 1973
Area: 20,167 m² (217,076 sq ft)

Used for sporting events and
concerts. The basketball game
between former NBA players and
the DPRK national team took place
here in 2014, as did the Mass Games
shown in the documentary film
A State of Mind.

Kumsusan Palace of the Sun
Location: Ryomyong Street
Date: 1976
Area: 10,700 m² (115,000 sq ft)

Formerly the official residence
of Kim Il Sung, and transformed
after his death into a mausoleum.
After the death of Kim Jong Il,
the palace was renovated again,
reopening in 2012 with both leaders
lying in state.

**Grand People's Study House
(overleaf)**
Location: Kim Il Sung Square
Date: 1982
Area: 100,000 m² (1,076,391 sq ft)

The central library and national
centre of Juche studies, located on
the central axis at the heart of the
city. It was conceived as part of
Kim Il Sung's aim to intellectualize
the whole of society.

Juche Tower

Location: Taedong River
Date: 1982
Height: 170 m (558 ft)

Located on the east bank of the
Taedong River, directly opposite
Kim Il Sung Square, the tower was
built to commemorate the leader's
70th birthday. The tapering, 150 m
(490 ft)-long granite spire, dressed
in white stone and capped with
an illuminated metal torch, is one
of the tallest in the world. At the
bottom is a statue of three figures
(opposite), who hold a hammer,
a sickle and a calligraphy brush,
which together form the insignia
of the Workers' Party of Korea.

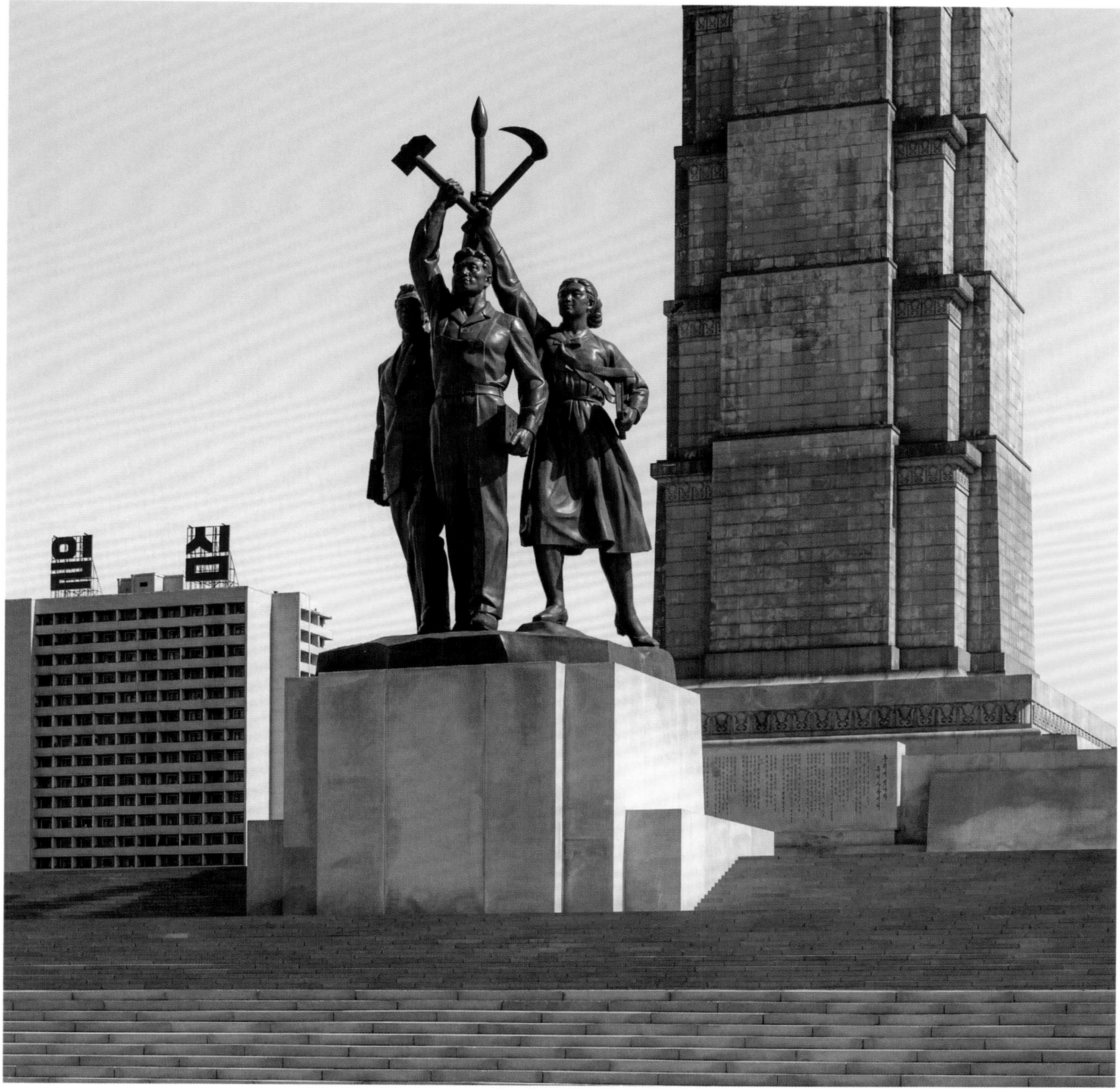
일
심

A mass dance in Kim Il Sung Square

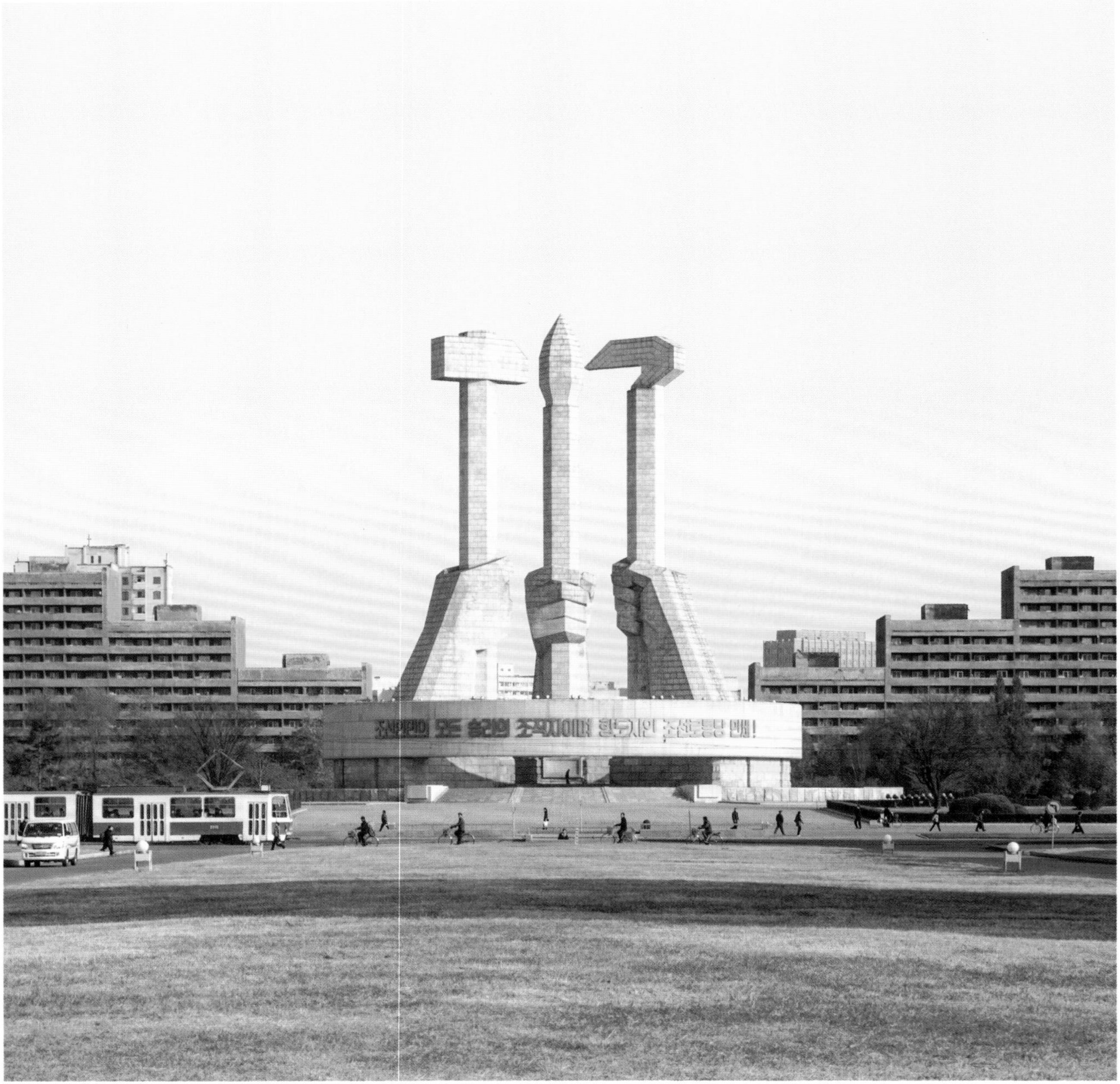

Monument to Party Founding

Monument to Party Founding
Location: Munsu Street
Date: 1995
Height: 50 m (164 ft)

The three fists holding a hammer, sickle and calligraphy brush (also seen on the Juche Tower; p. 126) represent the workers, farmers and intellectuals: the three segments of society in the DPRK. The height in metres represents the 50th anniversary of the founding of the Workers' Party of Korea, while the 216 blocks that comprise the belt and the 42 m (138 ft) inner diameter refer to Kim Jong Il's birthday: 16 February 1942. The buildings that previously stood between the monument and the river were demolished to free the visual axis to the Mansu Hill Grand Monument, which then extends to the Ryugyong Hotel.

Pyongyang Station
Location: Yokjon Street
Date: 1958
Area: 10,700 m² (115,000 sq ft)

The country's main railway station,
with connections to China and
Russia via its west and east coast
rail links. While there is a physical
route to Seoul, there is no service.
The station was rebuilt in 1958,
after the Korean War.

East Pyongyang Grand Theatre
Location: Munsu Street
Date: 1989
Area: 62,000 m² (670,000 sq ft)

The New York Philharmonic
performed here in 2008, the first
significant cultural visit to the DPRK
by the US since the Korean War.
The original façade and most of the
interior decoration were lost after
a fire in 2005.

Pyongyang Circus (overleaf)
Location: Kwangbok Street
Date: 1989
Area: 54,000 m² (581,250 sq ft)

Hosting numerous athletic events,
and appearing in several films, the
building was renovated in 2015. Much
of the interior design, including the
terrazzo floors and mosaics depicting
acrobats, were replaced with marble
and plaster neoclassical decorations.

Central Youth Hall
Location: Munsu Street
Date: 1989
Area: 59,900 m² (644,758 sq ft)

The design, chosen by Kim Jong Il
during an internal competition in 1986,
is defined by the red roof elements,
which represent an open piano
and an accordion. The main theatre
is beneath the 'piano', while an
auditorium is below the 'accordion'.

Pyongyang Ice Rink
Location: Chollima Street
Date: 1982
Area: 25,000 m² (269,000 sq ft)

Seating 6,000 and modelled on the
design of a skater's helmet, the
Pyongyang Ice Rink is one of the most
recognizable buildings in the city.
The Paektusan Prize International
Figure Skating Festival is held here
every February.

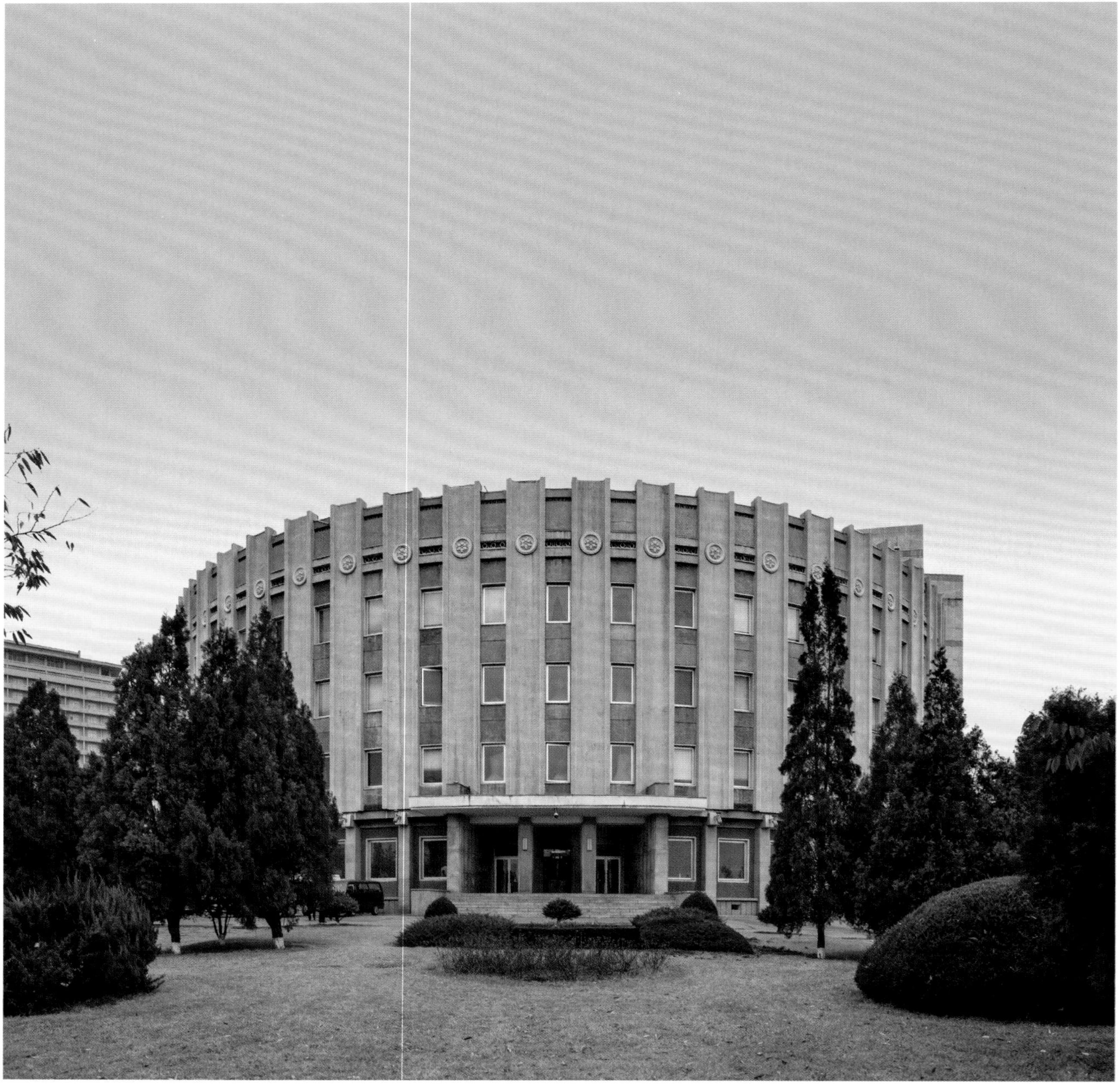

Changgwang Health Complex

Changgwang Health Complex
Location: Chollima Street
Date: 1986
Area: 37,548 m² (404,163 sq ft)

The shape of the building is the result of the addition of a beauty salon (circular in plan), a spa (square) and a swimming pool (rectangular). The design is a local variation of socialist modernism, a sort of 'brutalist decorativism', with surprisingly colourful interiors that feature tiles, glass bricks, mosaics, marble and wallpaper. The terrazzo floor in the circular entrance lobby depicts the Kimilsungia and Kimjongilia flowers (the latter a type of begonia), representing the former leaders. The health complex is open 16 hours a day, and can be used by up to 16,000 people at any one time.

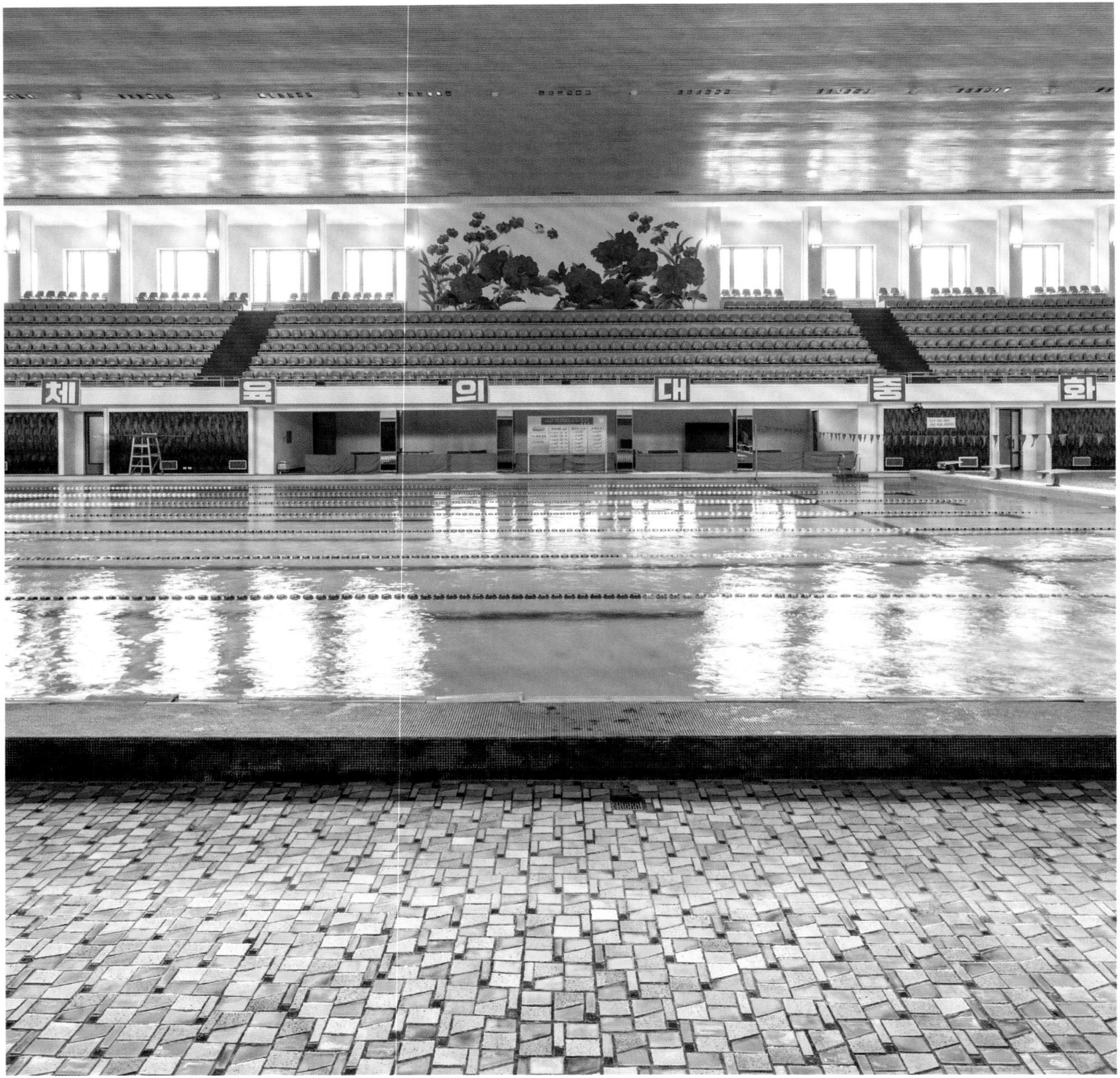
체육의 대중화

May Day Stadium
Location: Rungra Island
Date: 1989
Area: 207,000 m² (2,228,130 sq ft)

Known primarily for hosting the famous Mass Games, this circular stadium, one of the world's largest at the time of construction, comprises 16 parabolic arches, which together create a continuous 60 m (197 ft)-long canopy that covers most of the stands. Owing to its strong design – representing a magnolia blossom floating on a river – the stadium is an iconic presence on the city skyline, particularly from the Chongryu Bridge. Following a recent renovation, the façade, originally white, was clad with orange tiles, while the traditional decoration of the interior has been replaced by a saturated palette of pastel colours.

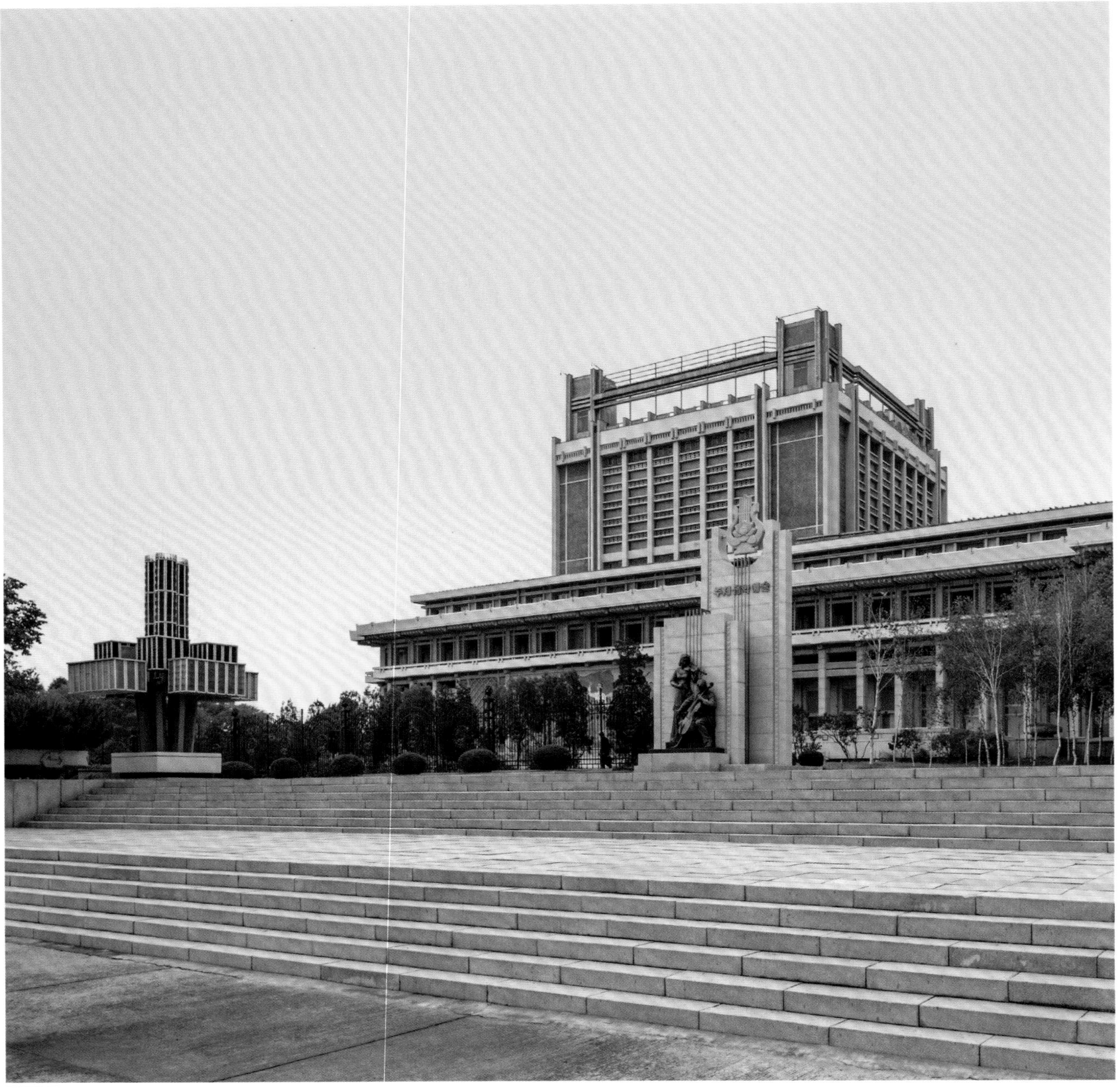

Mansudae Art Theatre

Mansudae Art Theatre
Location: Somun Street
Date: 1976
Area: 17,800 m² (191,600 sq ft)

The design somehow manages
to be both brutalist and highly
decorative, and serves as a stark
counterpoint to the Grand People's
Study House (p. 123), which lies
opposite. The sculpture features
28 women performing 'Snow Falls'.

Kaeson Cinema
Location: Moran Hill
Date: 1992
Area: 1,800 m² (19,375 sq ft)

The Kaeson Cinema is a popular
venue, owing to its location in the
city centre, next to a metro station.
Originally even more brutalist and
utilitarian in design, the building
was renovated in 2012. Films are
only shown in the daytime.

Kaeson Cinema

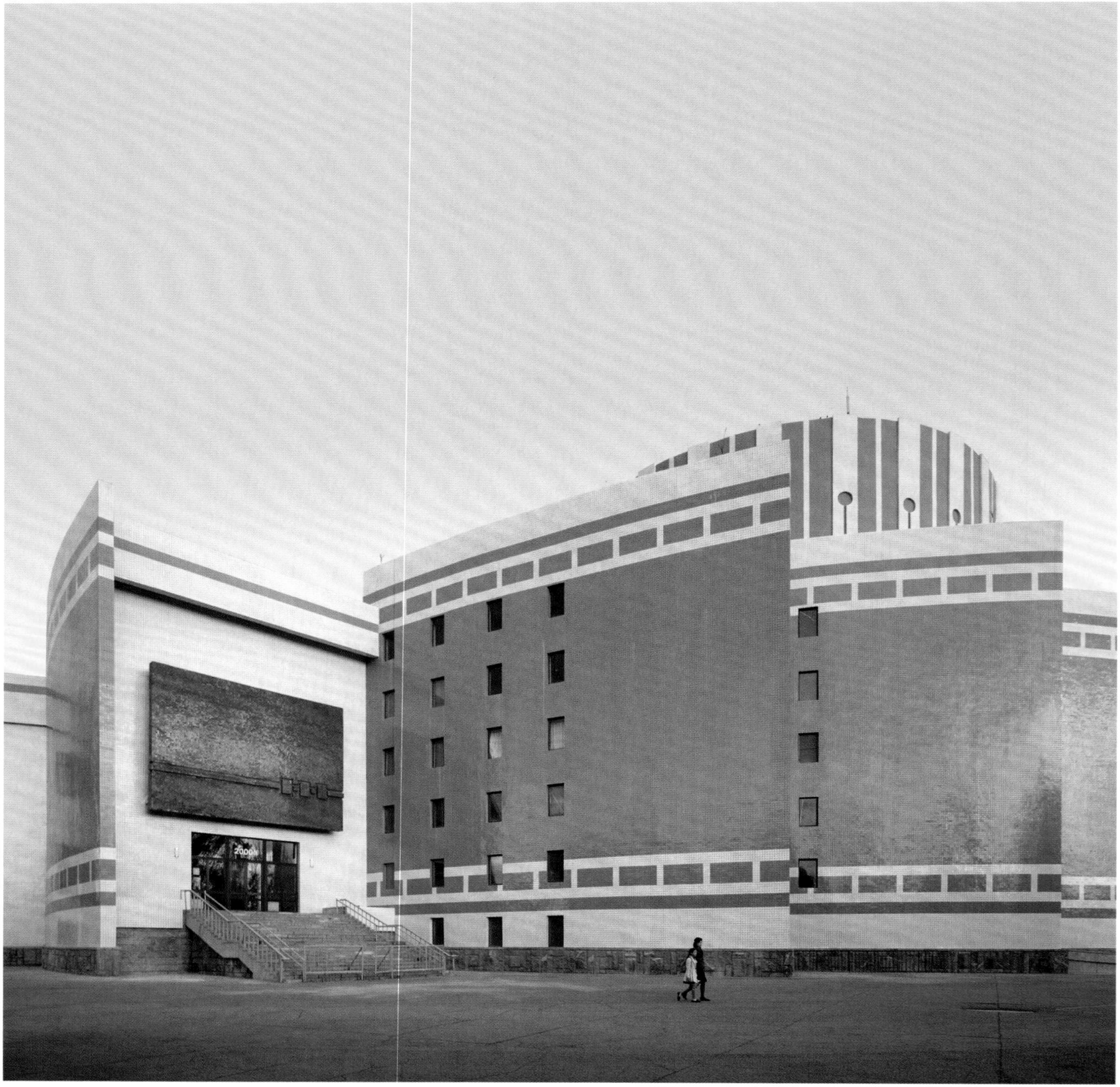

International Cinema Hall

International Cinema Hall
Location: Yanggak Island
Date: 1995
Area: 13,200 m² (142,084 sq ft)

The country's primary centre for
film, art and culture, all of which
were intensively promoted by
Kim Jong Il. Since 1987, it has also
hosted the biennial Pyongyang
International Film Festival, one
of the few events in the DPRK
that actively seeks connection
with the outside world. The
original concrete façade has
been covered in grey and white
ceramic tiles, reminiscent of
a film reel. The interiors have
been mostly left in their original
design, although one of the halls
has been recently upgraded
with up-to-date equipment and
a 'cinema bar', the first of its kind
in the city.

Yanggakdo International Hotel
Location: Yanggak Island
Date: 1995
Area: 87,870 m² (945,825 sq ft)

The design of the hotel was dictated by the triangular plot of land on which it sits, on an island south of the city centre, facing the Taedong River. This, together with the building's height, ensure that it is a landmark and reference point from across the city. It was built by the French company Campenon Bernard Construction, and has two external glass lifts and a revolving restaurant at the top with panoramic views of the city.

Koryo Hotel

Location: Changgwang Street
Date: 1985
Height: 143 m (469 ft)

The sci-fi silhouette of the hotel's twin towers (only one is open) is one of the most recognizable sights in Pyongyang. With 500 guest rooms, five restaurants, a swimming pool, two cinemas and a three-storey hidden suite, accessible only via a private lift, the Koryo Hotel is the second-largest working hotel in the DPRK and is generally seen as the 'business' hotel, while the entertainment-focused Yanggakdo (previous pages) is the largest and is considered the 'tourist' hotel. The façade, clad in glazed ceramic tiles, is original; the interiors have been partially renovated, with the warm tones of wallpaper, fabric and bronze replaced by colder white marble.

Chongnyon Hotel

Location: Kwangbok Street
Date: 1989
Height: 120 m (400 ft)

Built for the World Festival of
Youth and Students in 1989, the
Chongnyon Hotel has 520 rooms
across 30 floors, and sits in a
picturesque location overlooking
Kwangbok and Chongchun streets.
Its design combines cylindrical
shapes with dart-like pinnacles, and
the façade is clad in glazed ceramic
tiles, their green colour reminiscent
of traditional celadon pottery. The
lobby, dominated by a cone-shaped
glass dome, leads to an outdoor
swimming pool, an unusual facility
in the city's hotels, along with
a burger restaurant.

Sosan Hotel (opposite)

Location: Chongchun Street
Date: 1989
Height: 103 m (338 ft)

The Sosan Hotel, also overlooking
Chongchun Street (the 'City of
Sports'), was built at the same time
as the Chongnyon Hotel, and has
30 floors and 510 rooms, along with
a driving range. The design of the
façade is similar to the Chongnyon,
and the cladding – glazed ceramic
tiles – is the same, although in a
terracotta colour, rather than green.

Mangyongdae Children's Palace
Location: Kwangbok Street
Date: 1989
Area: 120,000 m² (1,300,000 sq ft)

This public facility provides a place for children to participate in after-school activities, from learning music, languages and computer skills, to playing games. It is the largest of such centres in the country, and contains 120 rooms, a swimming pool, a gymnasium and a 2,000-seat theatre. The design represents two curved wings, outstretched to encircle the plaza, symbolizing the embrace of the children by the leaders. The building was renovated in 2015: while the façade appears largely unchanged, the interior, originally quite sober and austere, has been transformed into an unexpectedly playful space filled with hyper-saturated colour.

The Subterranean Monument

The two routes of the Pyongyang metro system – the Chollima and Hyoksin lines –
were built between 1965 and 1973, and extended in 1987 to include 16 stations.
Tourists were originally only allowed to visit two of these, but today can visit every
station in the network. With a depth of 110 m (361 ft), the metro has a constant,
year-round temperature of 18° C (64° F). Staff wear military-style uniforms, and
Rodong Sinmun, the official newspaper of the Workers' Party of Korea, is displayed
in the stations, each of which has a different decorative scheme highlighting the
achievements of the DPRK (Hwanggumbol Station, for example, is decorated with
scenes of agriculture; see p. 169). Striking murals reinforce the message that the
metro was built 'with our own technique, our own materials and our own efforts';
some of these show Kim Il Sung providing 'on-the-spot guidance' to the workers.

Puhung Station

PYONGYANG NEXT

Since Kim Jong Un assumed leadership in 2012, Pyongyang has undergone a period of intense transformation, shaped by his vision for a new architectural direction. The result, with its futuristic, toy-like shapes and exuberant palette of pastel colours (most recently, Ryumyong Street), has led to an unexpected and thoroughly original urban environment – a declaration of intent by a city whose gaze is fixed firmly on the future.

문수거리

PLANS & DRAWINGS

Pyongyang

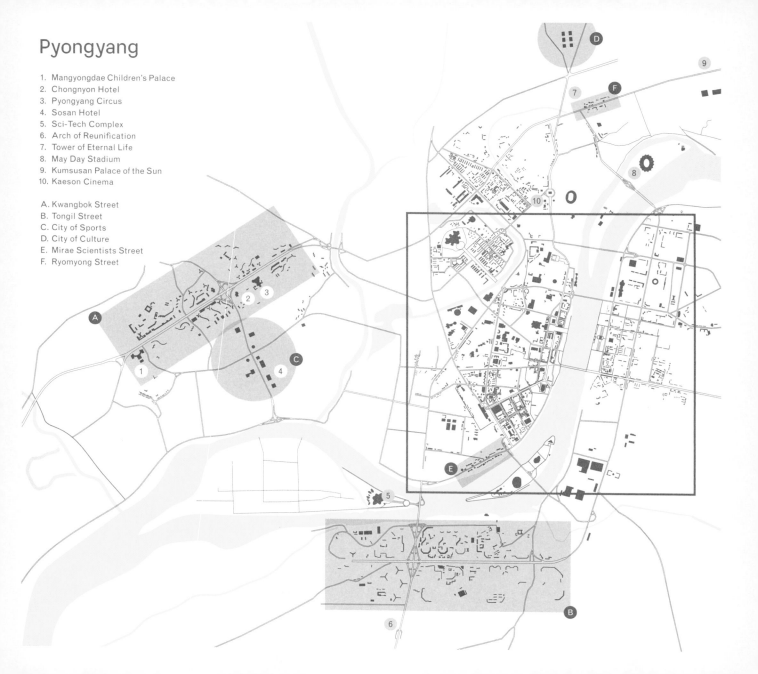

X. Axis 1
Y. Axis 2
Z. Axis 3

11. Ryugyong Hotel
12. Changgwang Health Complex
13. Pyongyang Ice Rink
14. Koryo Hotel
15. Pyongyang Station
16. Potong Gate
17. Mansudae Art Theatre
18. Grand People's Study House
19. Mansu Hill Grand Monument
20. Kim Il Sung Square
21. International Cinema Hall
22. Yanggakdo International Hotel
23. Juche Tower
24. Central Youth Hall
25. East Pyongyang Grand Theatre
26. Monument to Party Founding

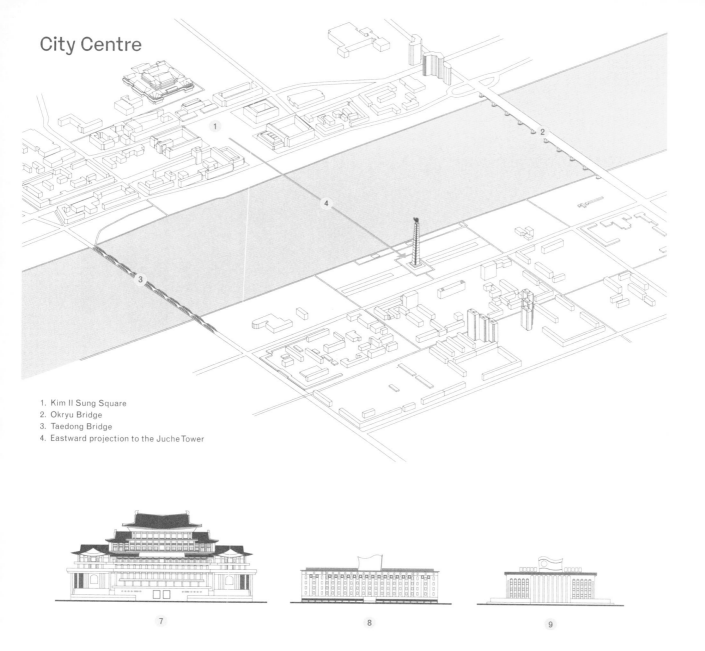

City Centre

1. Kim Il Sung Square
2. Okryu Bridge
3. Taedong Bridge
4. Eastward projection to the Juche Tower

7

8

9

Kim Il Sung Square

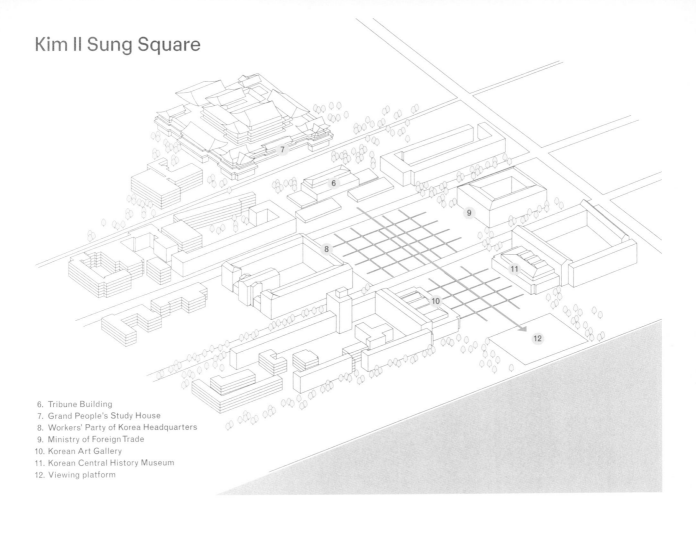

6. Tribune Building
7. Grand People's Study House
8. Workers' Party of Korea Headquarters
9. Ministry of Foreign Trade
10. Korean Art Gallery
11. Korean Central History Museum
12. Viewing platform

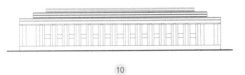

10

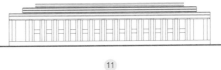

11

Mansu Hill Grand Monument

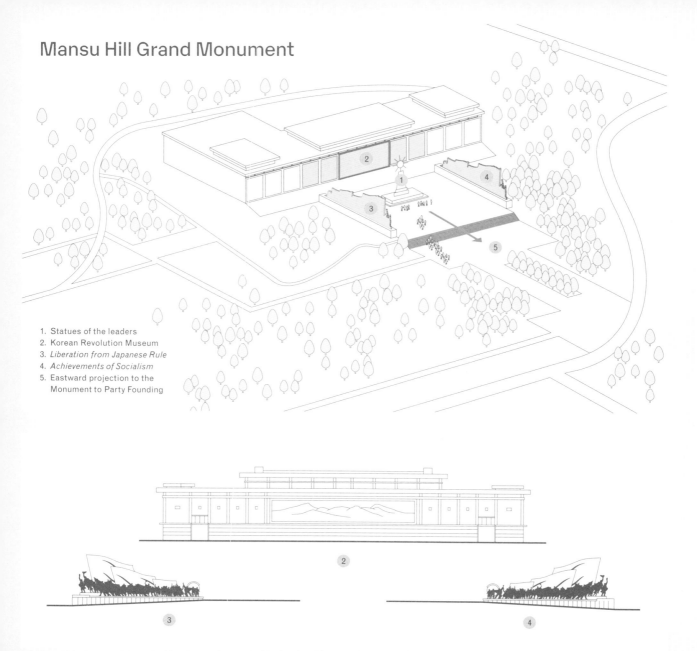

1. Statues of the leaders
2. Korean Revolution Museum
3. *Liberation from Japanese Rule*
4. *Achievements of Socialism*
5. Eastward projection to the
   Monument to Party Founding

Axis 1   Mansu Hill Grand Monument to the Monument to Party Founding

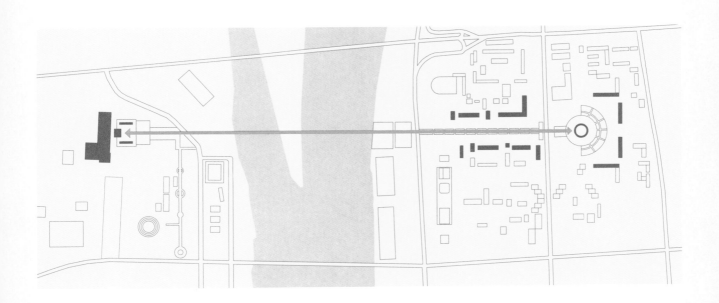

Axis 2 Kim Il Sung Square to the Juche Tower

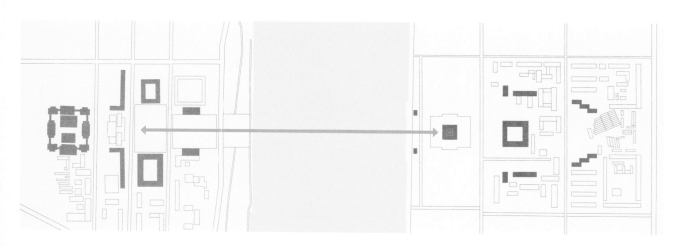

Axis 3 Potong Gate to Ryugyong Hotel

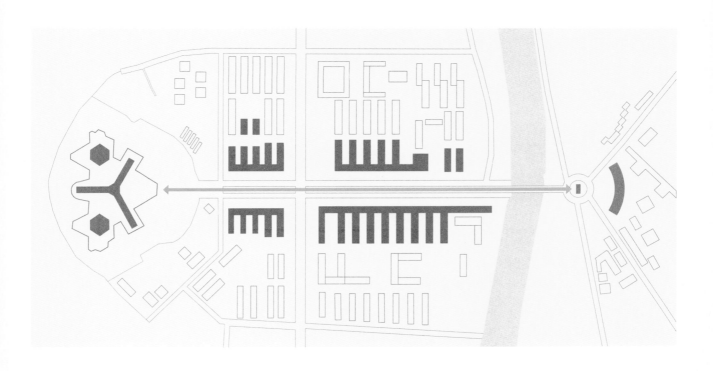

City of Culture Three Revolutions Exhibition

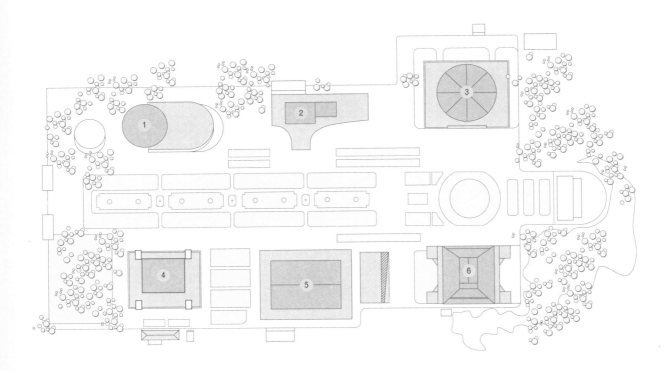

1. Electronics Industry Hall
2. Light Industry Hall
3. Agricultural Hall
4. General Introduction Hall
5. Heavy Industry Hall
6. New Technology Development Hall

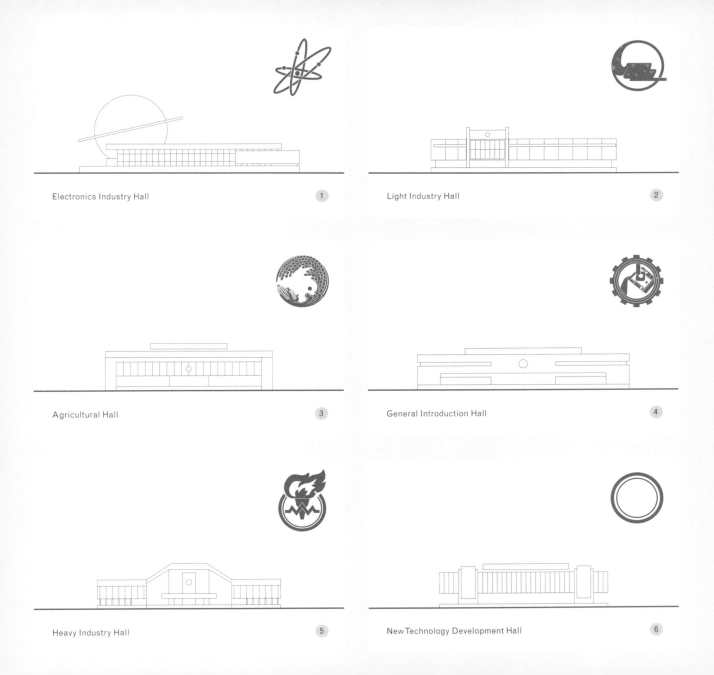

Electronics Industry Hall   1

Light Industry Hall   2

Agricultural Hall   3

General Introduction Hall   4

Heavy Industry Hall   5

New Technology Development Hall   6

City of Sports Chongchun Street

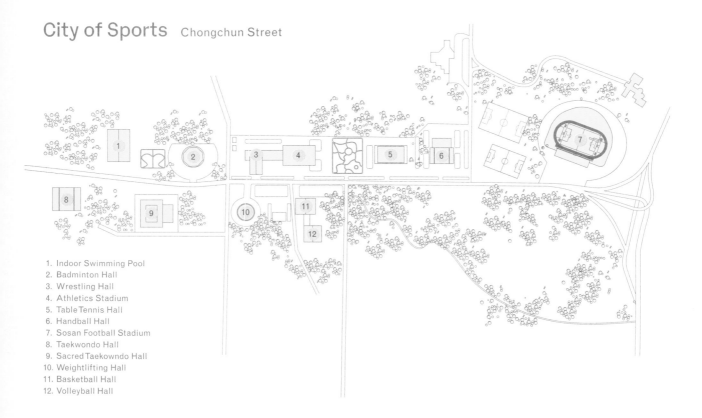

1. Indoor Swimming Pool
2. Badminton Hall
3. Wrestling Hall
4. Athletics Stadium
5. Table Tennis Hall
6. Handball Hall
7. Sosan Football Stadium
8. Taekwondo Hall
9. Sacred Taekowndo Hall
10. Weightlifting Hall
11. Basketball Hall
12. Volleyball Hall

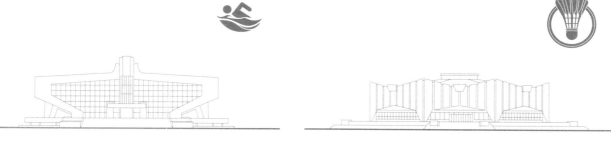

Indoor Swimming Pool

Badminton Hall

Wrestling Hall 3

Athletics Stadium 4

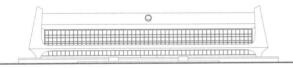

Table Tennis Hall 5

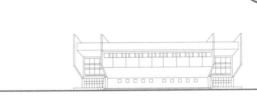

Handball Hall 6

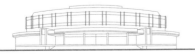

Weightlifting Hall 10

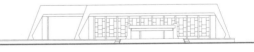

Basketball Hall 11

Tongil Street

Kwangbok Street

Kwangbok Street Building Typologies

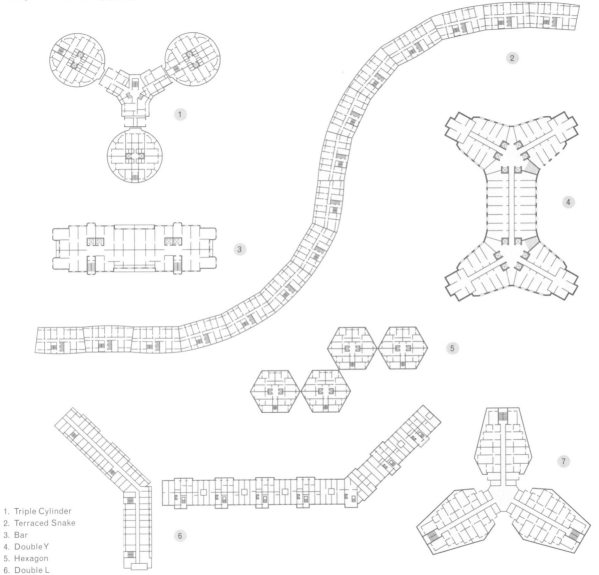

1. Triple Cylinder
2. Terraced Snake
3. Bar
4. Double Y
5. Hexagon
6. Double L
7. Windmill

Icons

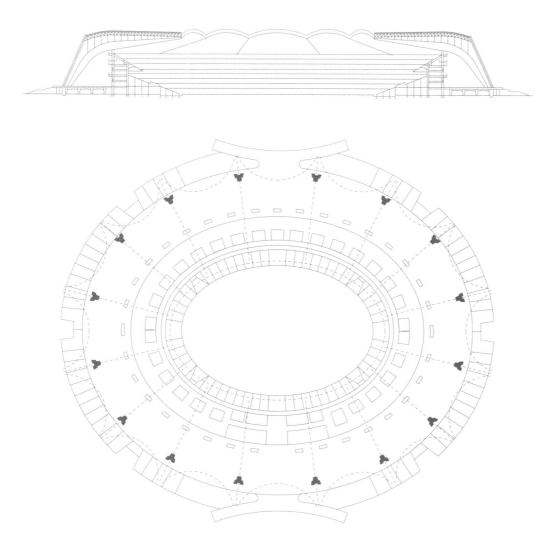

May Day Stadium

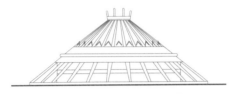

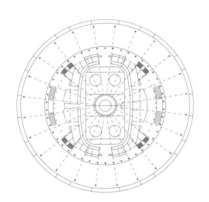

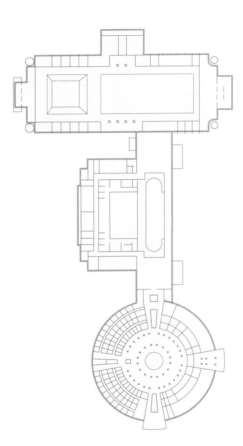

Pyongyang Ice Rink

Changgwang Health Complex

Icons

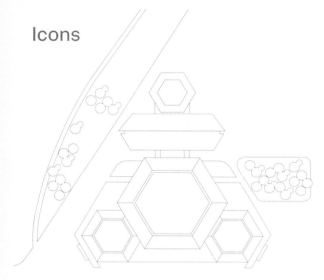

Pyongyang Circus

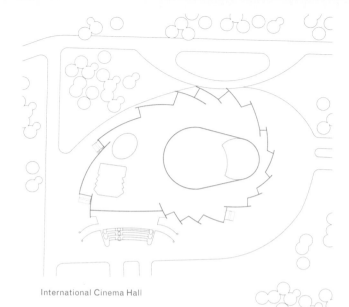

International Cinema Hall

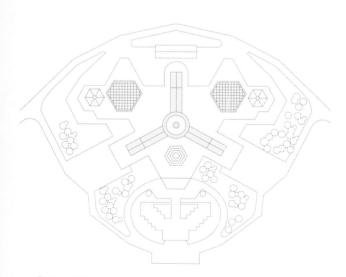

Ryugyong Hotel

Yanggakdo International Hotel

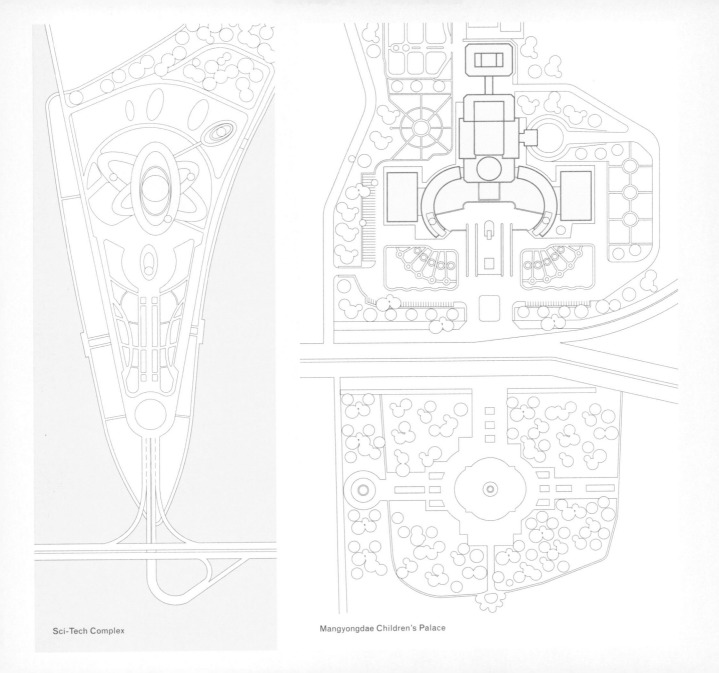

Sci-Tech Complex

Mangyongdae Children's Palace

Relative Scale

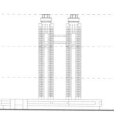
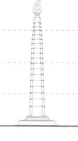

Pyongyang Ice Rink   Arch of Reunification   Koryo Hotel   Juche Tower

Metro station configurations

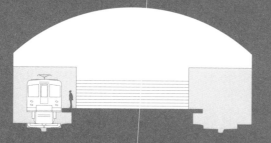

Puhung (Rehabilitation) Station

Hwanggumbol (Golden Fields) Station

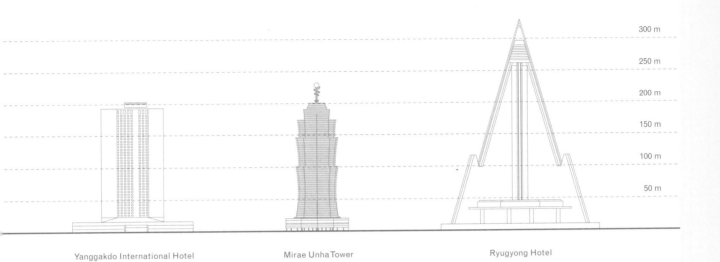

Yanggakdo International Hotel

Mirae Unha Tower

Ryugyong Hotel

300 m

250 m

200 m

150 m

100 m

50 m

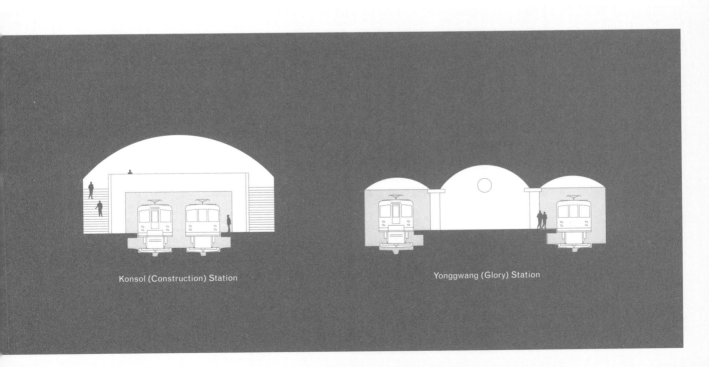

Konsol (Construction) Station

Yonggwang (Glory) Station

Pyongyang: 1993 to the Present
Nick Bonner and Simon Cockerell, Koryo Studio

Pyongyang is both the seat of national power and a showcase for the splendour of socialist architecture, North Korean-style – the face of the country to the outside world and a signifier of how it views itself. Citizens from across the DPRK visit the city in delegations and tour groups, to be enlightened and inspired by the museums, theatres and public spaces. At Koryo Tours, founded in 1993 and based in Beijing, we also provide access to this most mysterious and intriguing of countries, specializing in group and independent tours to the DPRK.

North Koreans are told that Pyongyang is one of the great cities of the world, built despite the difficulties the republic has been subjected to since its inception. To be a resident is to be placed in a utopia in which all of your political and social needs are fulfilled, the most fortunate among those already fortunate to be Korean. Everywhere in the city references to the State, the Party, or the Revolution are present, from grand mosaics depicting revolutionary scenes to illuminated slogans beaming mottoes such as 'one hundred battles, one hundred victories' (overlooking the Monument to the Party Foundation) or 'single-hearted unity' (on either side of the Juche Tower, the primary example of architecture as political symbolism).

Origins
Korean mythology asserts that Pyongyang was founded in 1122 BC, on the burial site of the of the legendary king Tangun. Although it has gone by a number of names over the years, the relevance of the term 'Pyongyang' is that it means 'flat land', being located on a small plain beneath hills. With the Taedong River providing for transport and trade, Pyongyang became the most important centre for political control in the northern part of the country. It was the capital of the Choson, Koguryo and Koryo kingdoms; in the 16th and 17th centuries, the city came temporarily under both Japanese and Chinese rule.

Despite various periods of invasion and upheaval across the centuries, Pyongyang maintained its core structure until the Korean War (known in the DPRK as the 'Victorious Fatherland Liberation War'), when it was almost entirely annihilated by a sustained bombing campaign. A mere handful of buildings survived, with most reduced to rubble. The destruction of the city continues to define the current political and social climate of the country, and local people are reminded of it incessantly by the education system and national media. While the postwar planners had a clean slate on which

(through museums such as the Victorious War Museum or the Mangyongdae Revolutionary Site) and subtly, via sculptures, mosaics and street propaganda. Iconic structures continued where space could be created, clearing 25 hectares for the Monument to Party Founding (1995), for example, or where development had not yet taken place, such as the May Day Stadium (1989) and the Yanggakdo International Hotel (1995). Significant anniversaries would also bring about waves of building: 1982 saw the erection of the Juche Tower to mark the 70th birthday of Kim Il Sung, and 2012, the year the leader would have been 100, the prestigious residential area of Changjon Street.

In the past decade there have been significant additions, including Mirae (2015) and Ryomyong (2017) streets. Extra floors were added to existing buildings, new towers erected for certain professions (university teachers, artistic performers), and commercial properties built. The renovation of interiors such as the Moranbong Theatre, Mangyongdae Children's Palace, Pyongyang Circus and Koryo Hotel are understandable, however much of the material used was imported and the qualities of the old interiors lost. Significant social impact was felt with the introduction of recognized and fixed-location markets, beginning in 2004 with Tongil Market, followed by various supermarkets aimed at the emergent middle classes – notably Kwangbok Department Store in 2011.

One thing that is widely known about Pyongyang is that it contains numerous monuments: concrete manifestations of power and ideology. The city can be seen simply as a piece of socialist art, which people happen to live in and around. It is often observed by visitors that the city is a largely 'empty' urban space, a theatre set with little non-planned intrusion or vernacular architecture. Yet more than three million people consider it home, and their lives interact with the city on a daily basis, however slight that impact may be.

The voice of the city
Pyongyang's working day begins with the morning public alarm (7am daily, although at a quieter volume on Sundays). People stream from their apartment blocks and head for work, the air filled with inspirational music, occasionally provided by school

to develop their masterplan, there was a clear palimpsest remaining. Owing, in part, to the surviving infrastructure and practicalities such as the rail network and constraints imposed by river crossings, there are still vestiges of streets left over from the ancient and prewar grids.

Function, or just form?
Pyongyang was rebuilt at speed, with the main avenues of the centre laid out, bridges renovated or new ones added, monumental architecture and utilitarian housing blocks created. The city operated as a space for living and working, and as a seat of power, the ideology instilled both directly

bands, out to instil 'revolutionary spirit' into the workers, just as they have since the Chollima Movement, the first industrial reconstruction campaign following the Korean War, in the 1950s. More recently, displays of synchronized flag-waving to encourage commuters and workers have become common, particularly during the recent 100- or 150-day labour campaigns, periods of intense activity known as 'battles'.

On construction sites, revolutionary songs and anthems blare out from speakers at high volume, the reach of the music holding primacy over clarity. The songs are interspersed with live-voiced, passionately delivered propaganda, from an assigned specialist in both 'news' and oration, seated in a specially modified van fitted with external speakers. These 'propaganda vans' can be seen on the streets of Pyongyang, travelling and bringing the latest news and policy to various sites throughout the day. Recordings of bells toll from Pyongyang Station at midday and midnight, as well as from the Grand People's Study House, overlooking Kim Il Sung Square. If traffic is light – as it often is – and the air still, they can be heard across the city.

More lights brighten the evening sky in the capital than in the past. Power shortages still exist, of course, but they are not as acute as they once were. One thing, however, remains guaranteed, regardless of blackouts, political tensions or whatever is going on in the world: the day ends as it always does, with the massive imitation flame atop the Juche Tower – the tallest stone tower in the world – being lit at dusk and extinguished at 11pm. The Mansu Hill Grand Monument, with its statues of Kim Il Sung and Kim Jong Il, remains illuminated throughout the night. Vehicles slow down as a sign of respect as they drive past. No darkness exists for this most politically sacred part of Pyongyang.

Transportation

While resident foreigners drive their own cars (with green registration plates) and tourists travel by bus or car, the local way of getting around the city remains by public transport or on foot. Bus, tram and trolley routes thread across the city, and the cost is almost comically low; just 5 won per journey, making it affordable for everyone (at the current exchange

rate, US$1 is approximately the equivalent of 9,000 won). The fabled metro system, one of the deepest and most ornate in the world, has two lines and 17 stations, and remains popular with travellers moving around the central and western parts of Pyongyang. No routes travel beneath the Taedong River to the eastern part of the city, despite plans for extensions having been drawn up long ago. There is often talk of expansion, and new stations in the western regions will open soon, but at the time of writing the most recent operational stations were built in the 1980s.

Since 2012, there has been a huge and highly visible increase in the number of taxis and taxi companies operating in Pyongyang. There were taxis before, but many did not have signs and were only identifiable by the fact that they were waiting in a certain location, or by their licence-plate numbers. Now companies such as KKG and Air Koryo maintain fleets of instantly recognizable vehicles that cruise the city for passengers from among the middle classes, who can afford them. A ride across town would set a passenger back a few dollars, many thousands of times more than using public transport, but something within economic reach of an increasing amount of the citizenry.

But despite this increase in a manifestly more bourgeois form of transport, it is still common to see long queues of people waiting for buses and trams during what passes for rush hour, as well as increased use of bicycles (and of better bicycles than in the past) on the designated cycle paths, confusingly laid out in the middle of pavements. Cyclists tend to be pretty law-abiding in Pyongyang, riding slowly and always dismounting at junctions, regardless of whether or not there is any road traffic, and pushing their bikes through pedestrian underpasses, instead of dashing across streets.

Rollerblades and mass parades

Kim Il Sung Square is the geographical centre of Pyongyang, the point from which the city radiates. It is used for the famous parades and rallies in which up to one million citizens and military personnel participate in an exhaustively rehearsed and tightly coordinated show, proceeding along the road atop the square (in front of the viewing platform) and continuing around

Provision of entertainment is seen as important, both as a leisure activity for the locals and for thrilling Koreans from the regions. Pyongyang has a famed circus, four fun-fairs and a water resort, Dolphinarium and ice rink; in the last decade, there has also been a surge in the construction of local parks, basketball and volleyball courts, skate parks (used for rollerblading, rather than skateboarding), all of which are in regular use. Sunday is the only official 'day off', and residents flock en masse to the Taedong River. Poets have devoted endless verses to the pleasure of boating here since the mid-14th century, and the river forms one of the historic 'Eight Views of Pyongyang' (each of which combines a location and an activity). Wedding parties pose for photos and young couples flirt in rickety rowboats. In 2016 the Taedonggang Beer Festival opened on its banks, and in the evenings the massive Taedonggang restaurant boat sets sail on the strip of water in front of Kim Il Sung Square.

Pyongyang prides itself on its generous amount of green space, claimed as the highest per capita in East Asia's capital cities. There are a multitude of small parks around the city, used for recreation, picnics and dancing. The main park, commonly visited by tourists and residents alike (there is a handy subway station and coach park at the main entrance), is Moranbong Park, the site of several of the 'Eight Views of Pyongyang'. A huge battle in the Sino-Japanese War (1894–95) and minor skirmishes during the Russo-Japanese War (1904–5) occurred here. One of the few places where propaganda is absent, the park is reserved for relaxation. On anniversaries and holidays, it becomes filled with families and groups of workers eating al fresco. This is a serious social event, a time to relax and a respite from the constraints of a rigorously ordered life. Moranbong Park is one of the truest forms of public space in the city.

the ministry buildings and from behind the bluff separating the square from the Taedong River (heightened as a flood barrier). Those in the square itself stand in pre-selected spots, marked by a dot of paint, and carry plastic double-sided flowers that can be used as a backdrop of Korean characters, spelling out whatever message is required, or to depict iconography such as the Workers' Party emblem.

These events occur less frequently than many outsiders would imagine, and for most of the year the square reverts to simply being an open space. But nature abhors a vacuum, and a common sight these days is children rollerblading, something that came into fashion a decade or so ago. This is not an organized activity, but an organic one to be celebrated. It is not unique to Kim Il Sung Square – skating takes place in many of the city's open spaces. Initially, skates would be rented from booths, but many children now have their own. Other facilities have popped up in public places, offering those with leisure time and money to spend the chance to use both. Shooting galleries (with pop-guns), snack kiosks, even lottery tickets, are all available in what are otherwise planned spaces – not planned for these activities, but used in this way nonetheless.

School is generally from 8am to 1pm, and children head to and from home unaccompanied, often from a very young age. For outsiders, is can be surprising to hear of everyday life they can relate to; one of the schoolgirls interviewed for the documentary film *A State of Mind* told us that she used to play truant in the mornings and head to Moranbong Park to play with her friends. Group life is the norm in the DPRK, and everyone is a member of one association or another, meeting for dancing, singing, playing cards, conversation or reading the news – even in such a quintessentially relaxing place as a public park, there is always some infusion of political life. Urban expansion is apparently well considered and green space is present in any new development, the most recent being a flower garden in the Mangyongdae District.

Use of the urban space

These activities straddle the line between formal and informal use of the available urban space. The latter has become much more common in the last decade, but in many ways, it was ever thus, just taking place in local neighbourhoods, in the courtyards between apartment buildings, hidden away from the main streets. This difference between public and semi-public is another characteristic of life in Pyongyang. It is only very recently that women have been allowed to ride bicycles in public, and there are still volunteer students who act essentially as fashion police, looking out for those who aren't dressed well enough to use the main thoroughfares. But in the semi-public sphere, people relax, chat, drink, fish, dress for comfort, gossip and live their lives.

Such space is used for drying chillies, playing cards, chatting with neighbours – social intercourse in a casual way. But the peripheries of such spaces are where the formal and informal meet: local communities are responsible for the upkeep of their housing blocks and localities, and communal efforts for maintenance and beautification are organized by neighbourhood committees. In recent years, there has been an increase in the planting of grass verges, which are maintained, cleaned and weeded by the residents. The near-invisibility of this part of life leads to the assumption commonly held by visitors that it simply isn't there. This is nothing more than a form of solipsism that does a great disservice to the people of Pyongyang, as they go about their lives away from the main streets of the city.

Although Pyongyang operates as a seat of power in which the revolutionary message is subtly and not so subtly infused into its citizens, it is also a city where people live, work, go to school, relax and chat with their friends. Officially, everything in North Korea is still government owned, however, with the economic changes of 2002, which kickstarted the normalization of forms of de facto private enterprise – within the context of the socialist macro-economy – the city functions more and more in ways that we, as outsiders, understand an urban space to function, with all of the various forms of social interaction that entails.

Building a Socialist Paradise   Oliver Wainwright

A pair of bright-green domes shines in the sun beneath a clear blue sky, emerging from the top of two cylindrical towers that rise from a plinth of shops with petal-shaped rooftops. A little further down stands another pair of gleaming shafts, square forms with bulbous turrets at each corner, shooting up from tapering conical bases like rockets ready for take-off. A third pair of towers, octagonal in form, recalls the pillars of ancient temples, banded with undulating ribbons of white balconies. The sequence continues for several blocks, with dozens of unusually shaped structures, symmetrically placed, creating a grand avenue that fades into the hazy distance.

This futuristic vision is Ryomyong Street, a complex of 5,000 apartments in towers of up to 70 storeys, which march down a vast new boulevard, lined with restaurants, green-grocers and drugstores – all things that have been a rare sight in the capital until recently. Translated as Sunrise Street (or 'the dawn breaks in the Korean revolution') and sited between the Kumsusan Palace of the Sun and the Ryonghung cross-roads, it is the latest grand urban project instituted by Kim Jong Un as a symbol of the reclusive state's economic pros-perity, defiant in the face of international sanctions.

'The completion of this street is more powerful than 100 nuclear warheads,' said Prime Minister Pak Pong Ju in a speech at the opening of the project in April 2017 – timed to mark the 105th birthday of Kim Il Sung, the country's founding father and Eternal President – to which 200 foreign journalists had been invited. Tens of thousands of Pyongyang residents also gathered in the street, some in military uniform, others in traditional suits and dresses, holding balloons, plastic flowers and North Korean flags, cheering ecstatically when the leader came to the stage.

Many of the foreign reporters were surprised by this vision of modernity, along with the claims of solar panels, geothermal heating and the use of green roofs and walls, but Ryomyong Street is just one of several such ambitious trophy projects that Kim Jong Un has been driving forward at speed since he came to power in 2012 and introduced the 'Strong and Prosperous Nation' policy. There are the glossy cylindrical towers of Changjon Street, standing like teetering stacks of coins, an 18-building complex rising to 47 storeys and nicknamed 'Pyonghattan' by foreign diplomats. There are the twin towers of housing for artists, their recessed balconies

inscribing pale blue spirals up the façades, giving them the look of cheerful sticks of seaside rock. There are several new areas built specifically for scientists, from the peach-coloured blocks of Unha Scientists Street to Satellite Scientists Street in Unjong District.

Mirae Scientists Street, located in Pyongchon District on the banks of the Taedong River, is one of the most exuberant developments of them all, and features a cluster of tapering orange and green apartment blocks, their curved forms apparently modelled on 'the shape of an intellectual's brush'. At the end of the street stands a gigantic landmark tower inspired by a great pagoda, its petal-shaped floors flaring out at steep angles, its summit crowned with a golden globe encircled by a silver spiral. Visible for miles around, it is one of the capital's most recognizable new landmarks, a retro sci-fi vision that could be straight from the pages of a Dan Dare comic.

In all of these new projects – which are officially said to be directed from the top, guided by the personal advice of Kim Jong Un – there is an explicit desire to embody a specifically Korean national identity, while simultaneously embracing the history and future of the DPRK. It is a campaign first begun by Kim Jong Un's father, Kim Jong Il, who laid out the principles for building the new nation in his 160-page treatise *On Architecture*.

into the capital construction sector adopted foreign designs mechanically, asserting their erroneous views, ignoring the country's economic situation and turning a deaf ear to the people's aspirations and demands. The reconstruction efforts left a city of 'European-style buildings ... which did not accord with our people's customs and sentiments'.

Kim Jong Il began a programme of construction that would be 'national in form and socialist in content', embodying his father Kim Il Sung's Juche ideology. It is a legacy that Kim Jong Un is clearly keen to carry on, in his own inimitable way. In his own architectural manifesto, *For Building a Thriving Nation*, published in 2016, he specifies that architects must strive to 'combine national identity properly with modernity, and build at an extraordinary speed monumental structures that will surpass global standards and remain immaculate, even in the distant future'. With his eye firmly set on the future, his new generation of buildings take historical motifs – the forms of octagonal columns and ancient pagodas – and dress them up in a range of futuristic costumes, employing high-tech tropes and explicitly modern materials.

Colour is a key part of this new architectural arsenal. As part of a programme begun under Kim Jong Il, and accelerated by Kim Jong Un, many of the tired concrete buildings in the capital have been painted in a pastel rainbow of chalky terracotta and mustard, turquoise and violet, while the interiors have been spruced up with candy-coloured synthetic finishes. Complementary colour palettes are often deployed, matching green with purple, blue with pink, salmon with teal, bringing a sense of exuberance and echoing the contrasting colours of the *Joseon-ot*, the traditional national dress. Glazed ceramic tiles are often used to clad the new towers, giving them an extra glossy sheen.

There has been an emphasis on ambitious new buildings for leisure and pleasure, too, catering to the emerging middle class of Pyongyang with money to spend. On Rungra Island in the Taedong River stands the People's Pleasure Ground, a theme park complete with pink-painted rollercoasters, mini-golf course, swimming pool and 4D cinema, fitted out with 'rhythmic' moving seats. At its heart is the Dolphinarium, a startling building shaped like a big white whale, where Chinese

'An architect who is convinced that his country and his things are the best,' he wrote, 'will not look upon foreign things or try to copy them, but make tireless efforts to create architecture amenable to his people.'

After the Korean War in the 1950s, when Pyongyang was flattened by US bombing, reconstruction work was mostly carried out by Soviet-trained architects, leaving a legacy of foreign influence that the leadership was keen to expunge in the following decades. 'In the difficult days after the war, when we had to start everything again from scratch,' Kim Jong Il continued, 'the sycophants, dogmatists and anti-Party counter-revolutionary elements that had wormed their way

dolphins perform somersaults on demand, leaping from a pool of saltwater that was pumped here from the sea along a 100-km (62-mile) pipeline. Nearby is the Munsu Water Park, a complex of brightly coloured looping slides and a wave pool, along with two indoor pools covered by a cluster of faceted glass pyramids. It could be Florida or Dubai, if it wasn't for the lifelike waxwork of Kim Jong Il, standing on an artificial beach in the lobby, wearing his trademark safari suit. The sci-fi comic-book urge reaches its peak in the Sci-Tech Complex (opposite), a science and technology centre built in the shape of an atom, with a vast glass dome surrounded by elliptical wings, following the shape of electrons swirling in orbit.

'Let us usher in a great golden age of construction by thoroughly applying the Party's Juche-orientated idea on architecture,' Kim Jong Un recently declared, unveiling plans for specialized science cities and tourist resorts with underwater hotels, all rendered in shades of pink and baby blue. 'Let us turn the whole country into a socialist paradise!'

While the country's previous leaders used architecture to build the city with a sense of timeless gravitas, Kim Jong Un's policies reveal more of an escapist urge. He seems intent on constructing a world of colourful, toy-like buildings to project an image of carefree prosperity, recasting Pyongyang as a stately pleasure dome for the world to envy.

On the cover: *front*, Ryugyong Hotel in 2015 (the wall in front of the building has since been removed); *back*, a mural in the entrance hall of the Paektusan Academy of Architecture.

Published by arrangement with Thames & Hudson Ltd., London, by the MIT Press

Model City Pyongyang
© 2019 Thames & Hudson Ltd, London
Text © 2019 Cristiano Bianchi
Photographs © 2019 Cristiano Bianchi
Drawings © 2019 Kristina Drapić
Foreword © 2019 Pico Iyer

ISBN 978-0-262-04333-5

Library of Congress Control Number: 2019933580

Printed and bound in China
by C & C Offset Printing Co. Ltd

The MIT Press
Massachusetts Institute of Technology
Cambridge, Massachusetts 02142
http://mitpress.mit.edu

Our deepest gratitude to Koryo Studio, especially to founder Nicholas Bonner, for his experience, hard work, contacts, resources, passion and humour, but most of all his friendship, and to Simon Cockerell, Adrian Sandiford, James Banfill and Vicky Mohiedden. Without them, this project would not have been possible.

Thanks are also due to Korea Cities Federation, who organized and managed our work in Pyongyang, and to Pico Iyer, Oliver Wainwright, Karen Smith, Riccardo Pallecchi and Dinamo Digitale, and the team at Thames & Hudson.

Last but not least, thank you to our families and all the friends who supported and inspired us, gave ideas and suggestions, reviewed numerous drafts, and through it all added technical and emotional depth to the project: Matjaž Tančič, Stefan Malešević, Miranda Vukasović, Nicola Saladino, Jelena Prokopljević, Giorgia Cestaro, Nemanja Radovanović, Federico Ruberto, Daniele Dainelli, Beatrice Leanza, Ting-I Tsai and Gabriele Battaglia. This book is dedicated to them.

Cristiano Bianchi is an architect, and the founder of Studio ZAG, which has offices in Tuscany and Beijing. His recent work in architectural photography is focused on the social and urban transformation occurring in Asia. He lives and works in Italy and China.

Kristina Drapić is a Serbian-born architect and graphic designer. She moved to Italy as a child, where she studied architecture and landscape design in Milan, before spending four years in China, studying the relationship between architecture, sociology and ideology. She lives in Belgrade.

Koryo Studio is the cultural department of Koryo Tours (koryotours.com), a British-run company, based in Beijing, specializing in travel in the DPRK. The firm also produces and promotes film, and artistic and cultural projects in Korea, owing to an expertise gleaned from monthly visits to the country since 1993.